Serious Shift

How Experience Delivery Can Save Your Practice

Meena.

SHIFT. SERIOUSLY.

Den.

DENNIS
MOSELEY-WILLIAMS

PAINTED BY RADAR INC.
Ottawa, Canada

ISBN 978-0-9919741-0-8
Printed in United States of America

Contents

This book is dedicated to my Mum.
Your generosity and capacity for love and compassion knows no bounds.
Not only do I love you, Mum, I wish I could be more like you.

Acknowledgments

I WISH TO PERSONALLY thank the following people for their inspiration, contributions to my knowledge and for help in creating this book.

When you do something important like win an Oscar or get elected to public office – or when you are celebrated or feted in any way – the very first people you wish to thank are those in your family. This is certainly true most of the time. However, I'm convinced that anyone who has ever written a book would tell you the first person you thank is your editor.

Susan Rothery has served as my editor, for which I am eternally grateful. Some of the time, she was also the writer. All of the time, however, she has been engaged and incredibly supportive. She not only made this project possible but also made it so much better than if she hadn't participated. Thanks, Susan – this was fun. Let's do it again now that we have it figured out.

Tom Frisby is the other half of DMWSC; he is also my friend and my business hero. Tom, your complete support from the start – your input, contributions and guidance – were invaluable to me while writing this book. Thank you for making my argument clear and concise. You have shed light into the corners.

To my wife Sherri: you were right all along. I *can* write a book. I don't know how I could possibly list all the things you do that I love, and I don't know how I could possibly pick only a few to mention here. You know what nobody else knows, girl, and I want to thank you for all of it. I don't know how somebody so amazing could have such horrible taste in fellas, but I am thankful for that too.

Introduction

I Am He as You Are He as You Are Me And We Are All Together

THE REASON I AM writing this book is because of my intent to help you become a finisher, understand resistance and live a life less ordinary.

Specifically, it is because of my intent to help financial advisors build a world-class wealth management practice that allows them to live a more fulfilling and personally satisfying life. I want to help those people who wish to bring a soul to their enterprise, who believe that their success comes not only from the sound professional advice and services they provide their clients, but also from the experience they deliver.

In my business, I do this a lot of different ways. I write blogs. I conduct workshops. I consult privately. Some of these methods are too expensive for some people, which is why I particularly enjoy blogging. It's free and it allows me to reach people who might otherwise not have access.

This book is like that. It is really my gift to you. I don't expect to make any money on it, and that isn't my intention anyway. My intention is to write the one book you actually need. I am not kidding myself; it's not literature. I doubt very much that, outside of my professional world, anyone I know will even realize I published it. I don't consider this book to be as impressive as any work of fiction, published or as yet to be published. But I do want someone to be able to say in twenty years, "Read this book." I would like my book to be one of the few 'how to' books that a person like you keeps on their shelf and periodically takes down to read just because of what is says.

I don't want to add pages simply to increase perceived value. One of the best business books I ever read was *The One-Minute Manager* by Ken Blanchard, and I don't think it took me more than an hour to read it.

So those are my reasons. What I think is more important, however, is the following question: why are you reading this book?

You will find this book helpful if you believe, as I do, that your success stems from your intent. That is to say, successful people are successful, first and foremost, because they intend to be a great person and do great things. Let me repeat that: the primary intention of most successful people is to help others, not to enrich themselves.

This isn't to say that I am not – or that successful people are not – motivated by and desiring to make more money. I only wish to stress that the desire to be great must come before the desire to be rewarded.

My goal is to inspire you to innovate or change yourself for the better, to hone your intent. My goal is to help you implement new behaviors and anchor them with discipline and process. I want to inspire you to make simple adjustments and apply simple systems so that you can realize a much more rewarding life personally and professionally.

My observation has been that very successful people make their achievement look effortless. I have studied them, I know how they do it, and I want to share that with you for all the right reasons. I want to help you. I'm that transparent.

So this book is meant to help you cut through all the nonsense, cut through all the things you could do but don't. Let's just agree that you want more clarity, not more information. Let's clean your shelves and digital libraries of all those crazy books, kits, tapes, podcasts, vodcasts, and first just get you started, get you accepting and embracing a simple strategy for living a successful life as a financial advisor.

But don't throw those tapes and things out yet – they will come in handy. Later, when you have time to enjoy them, you can make a coffee, sit in a big comfortable chair in a place you love, and enjoy them. For now, though, they are in the way.

There you have it. Those are my goals for this book and for you. I want you to be able to read it and immediately take action to innovate and implement meaningful and lasting change in your business and your life.

WHAT KIND OF PRACTICE DO YOU WANT TO RUN?

I would like to share what I would consider a successful practice. This is my inspiring vision of success.

I think a really nice practice would be a fee-based business with 100 million dollars under management and 150 clients (a 'client' being a person or a family) who feel I am indispensable to them. I want my clients to value my counsel and appreciate my friendship. The practice runs smoothly, it is in a great space, is very comfortable and fun. Everyone on my team feels connected and fulfilled. They take a lot of pride and feel well-rewarded for their service.

Clients love coming to my office because they feel it is an event, something they can look forward to, learn from and talk about. Clients feel well prepared before our meetings. They appreciate the décor, the obvious effort we have invested in making them feel comfortable. I have a coffee maker inspired by Rube Goldberg that you have to fire up with a pull cord, and when you do, birds scatter in the trees outside.

My clients receive a financial planning stewardship experience that cannot be duplicated by anyone. They are informed about their investments because I have educated them. They refer people to me because they want their family and friends to be taken care of. I am in a position to be very selective about the people I spend my time with.

In this envisioned workplace, I love what I do. I love going to work, but I also really love to have fun, spend money and go and see things. That's life, and it's going by fast, so I intend to make the most of it.

I have earned the right to do this because I have done a lot of other things right. So here's the thing: I want to make sure you can do this too, or do more of this, right away.

We both have to agree, though, that for this to be your reality, you have to build a sustainable business. A sustainable business means it can be maintained. You have to commit to what you are doing. This isn't a campaign. We are not trying to get excited about selling more cars before the deadline so that we might win a turkey or a golf club. We are not interested in getting busier for a little while. We want to get better, forever. Meaningful change is lasting change.

What you will discover as you read this book is that if you want to enjoy being the CEO of a world-class wealth management business, then you have to build it yourself.

From here on in, I'd like you to adopt what is known in Buddhist circles as beginner's mind. Successful advisors (and even non-advisors) never assume they have all the answers, and they never assume they are right. They are always listening for insight on how they can make what they do better. Try to avoid the trap of its opposite, expert's mind. As you might expect, adherents of this practice think they know everything, and these people are the hardest to help. They have shut themselves off from opportunity.

We are setting your sails here. We are choosing where you are headed, and we are laying down the big pieces to get you moving towards it. Later on in the voyage, when you are under sail and things are proceeding smoothly, we'll go over the entire operation. We'll fill in some things, smooth over other things, and we'll make even better progress. But for now, you only have to commit to getting out of the harbour, on course and on the way.

Chapter 1

Who Are They, and How Do They Do It?

I HOPE YOU ARE AN entrepreneur because being an entrepreneur is the single greatest lifestyle in the world.

Entrepreneurs create something out of nothing. They are artists, they are producers, they are musicians, they are factory owners, they are caterers. They open print shops and bake shops, own restaurants and dry-cleaning services. They are fashion designers and model train retailers, and they are financial advisors. Yes, they are you.

They create industry and take risks. They innovate, they expend energy, they seize the day. At one end of the spectrum, they can be one-trick ponies, and at the other end, they can be transformative. Think Apple, think Google, think Henry Ford.

Very successful financial advisors (or VSAs) take an entrepreneurial approach to running their businesses. They fully commit to their business and see it as their craft, their art, their passion. They regard their business as a work in creation, constantly being directed and developed, something that demands their unique stamp, their vision.

They do not emphasize products, they stress process and experience.

They focus completely on improving the enjoyment and delivery of the experience they provide to their clients.

They also make it look very easy. More often than not, VSAs build process-driven practices that have committed to fulfilling a simple obligation. That obligation is typically the delivery of a superior client experience.

VSAs network easily. Their phone rings because people prefer to call them to solve problems or to seek out their opinions. VSAs don't need to worry about acquiring new clients or referrals. People ask them for help all the time.

The word that keeps coming to mind is *natural*. VSAs make it look easy, even though they work hard at it.

I have worked closely with very successful financial advisors for at least fifteen years now, and the following observation is as true today as it was when I started: VSAs are actually very disciplined people who are guided by an enlightened set of ideals. Furthermore, I've found that what makes them so successful isn't difficult to understand or duplicate. It's all a matter of intent and an unrelenting focus on the big picture.

IDEALS, INTENT – WHAT DOES THAT MEAN?

The initial intention of VSAs for being in business is their desire to help others, not to enrich themselves. VSAs make their intention an obligation, and they build their business around fulfilling it.

Here is an example. Starbucks didn't start out with the intention of selling a lot of coffee. They started out with the intention to create "the third place." Starbucks identified the need for and the opportunity to provide an environment that was comfortable and inviting, a shared space and community hub where – after one's home and workplace – a person could go to enjoy a bit of community and company with a fantastic cup of coffee.

What Starbucks believed was that if you created a better experience and provided a superior cup of coffee – one that could be customized and fancied up – and furthermore, if you put that coffee experience in a nice space that offered some peace in an otherwise busy world, then they would sell more coffee than anyone else, at a premium price.

Starbucks didn't put other shops out of business so much as they proved that there was a desire and a market for this kind of experience. The result? Starbucks set the new standard.

Incidentally, you would probably enjoy reading *The Starbucks Experience* by Joseph Michelli, a comprehensive examination of the company's business strategies and reasons behind its creation.

Starbucks' intention was to create a superior, completely customizable product within a relaxing environment that would add value to each customer's day. Every corporate decision Starbucks made was ultimately measured against the following statement: "We inspire people one sip, one cup, and one neighbourhood at a time." So every strategy and every investment they considered was measured against this statement with the question, "Does this help us do that?"

As a result, they have taken every step necessary to ensure they continue to innovate around that idea.

Did putting an insulated sleeve on a hot cup help them do that? Absolutely. I can vaguely remember the first time I experienced one, and I am sure that I said, "What a great idea." That little sleeve is consistent with Starbucks' intention of changing people's lives. How did they make drinking their coffee a better experience? By stopping the pain. Literally.

That simple sleeve was also a brilliant innovation. Anyone could have come up with the idea of it if they were thinking the right way. Starbucks was thinking about experience, and they were driven by a higher goal than just selling units. I really don't believe that Starbucks would have innovated around the insulated sleeve had they not been thinking right in the first place.

So your intention is to create an experience that educates and empowers investors to make the best decisions possible. Your purpose is to serve as a Personal CFO to a select group of investors and their families, to help them live remarkable lives. Are you going to be invited to weddings and funerals? Are people going to trust you and thank you for your advice? Are you going to make the short list of indispensable people in their lives?

Or are you going to try to sell them more stuff?

If you are trying to be the best version of yourself, then you want to do all that you can to be anything other than someone who is seen as a salesperson or a product specialist. When you are seen as a product specialist or a salesperson you risk that your perceived value is tied to returns, and your clients may not see the value of the full picture – that holistic, encompassing process you bring to the relationship through your intention and professionalism. You want your clients' trust more than anything else, and your focus and intent must be on creating that trust.

So ask yourself: is your intention to help people or to close people?

When you are able to articulate exactly what you do and exactly why you do it, you can then make this new purpose your obligation and build a business that delivers on this obligation.

INTENTION LEADS TO ALIGNMENT AND AUTHENTICITY

You are looking to align what you want to do with what you actually do, with more people who want it done and who want it done the way you do it.

Stitch that on a pillow.

When the experience you deliver isn't aligned with the experience you want to deliver, you have no alignment. When you are not offering solutions to the specific problems your ideal clients have, then you are out of alignment, and your success will be sporadic at best. When you understand what you want to do and for whom, and you build a practice around that obligation, then you attract clients.

Here is a staggering truth: most financial advisors walk around unclear about what they actually do. Look how similar they all are. Look at the same approach they take to the same problems. Almost every single advisor struggles with process and with generating referrals. Why?

I suspect the reason is because they all think the same way, and they resist the truth because the entrepreneurial side of things doesn't necessarily match up with what they do best.

Maybe it's because they are all thinking about how 50 million dollars breaks down into clients. One client at $50 million. Or two clients at $25M, or maybe ten at $5M, or maybe as many as 50 with assets between $500K and $3 million, or...

That is not what you should be thinking about. You should be thinking about what kind of client you want to work with. You should be thinking about what kind of solutions that person needs, and you should focus on creating a client experience that is aligned with those two objectives. Think about them as people, not portfolios. You get along with people, some better than others. Portfolios, on the other hand, are just paperwork.

Once you have figured out what it means to be aligned with your clients, then you need to ensure that all expressions of that alignment are authentic, meaning that they are genuinely felt and expressed by you and every member of your team. Your clients respond to interactions and events that are engaging, personal, memorable and transparent, and they will sense insincerity in a heartbeat.

Once again, if you intend to own a world-class wealth management practice, then you will need to build it yourself.

IF YOU BUILD IT THEY WILL COME

I believe that the efforts of a practice should be focussed 20% on the financial aspects and 80% on the development and enhancement of relationships with existing and potential clients. When you accept a new client into your practice, how often does the new client cite poor returns as a reason for straying from their previous advisor? More often than not, they point to the lack of relationship, clarity of process or the lack of connection.

Granted, you most certainly have to make them money. I am not suggesting that rate of return is not important to your clients. It's very important. However, there is a need for clarification.

First, the only benchmark that you need to teach your clients to be concerned with is the benchmark set by their own financial plan. For example, their plan might stipulate that for that client to retire, he or she must achieve an annual rate of return of 7.2%. That is what your client should care about. He should not care about what the Dow Jones is doing because you've taught him not to. You have framed the perspective your client has on that information. The only reason many investors actually do care about the Dow Jones is because their financial advisor has done a horrible job of clarifying and explaining what their personal benchmark is as determined by their plan.

Secondly, if your client feels that they have no personal connection with you, or you with them, or if they feel that you are difficult to understand or sporadic with your communication, they will not be satisfied with returns alone.

As you will see throughout this book, this is an experience business built on relationships. Your clients have to feel that you understand them and are connected with them.

Very successful advisors believe that the experience they deliver is as important as the returns they generate. These advisors not only connect with the investor – their goals, concerns, and financial realities – but they clearly make a concerted effort to know and understand the client.

What successful, entrepreneurial advisors understand is that clients have to feel that you empathize with them. People are people; we all like having someone in our corner, and we all like to do business at places where we feel we are appreciated. I feel this way about my tailor, my mechanic and the shop owners along my street. I am truly convinced that I get more out of the experience of knowing them because I feel that I have a relationship with them. The same holds true with my butcher, baker and the owner of the Mexican restaurant a block over. I use these examples to make the point that getting to know your customers/clients creates authentic relationships that lead to loyalty.

So naturally, this is true when I consider the person who manages my financial well-being. It's better for both of us, in good and bad markets, to feel connected and partnered. It's dangerous for any advisor whose clients simply see them as the purchaser of securities.

Seth Godin wrote in one of his blogs that, "It's easier to love a brand when the brand loves you back,"[1] and I think that pretty much sums it up.

---

[1] Seth Godin, http://sethgodin.typepad.com/seths_blog/2012/07/its-easier-to-love-a-brand-when-the-brand-loves-you-back.html (July 15, 2012).

EMPATHIZE AND COMMUNICATE

An industry study that polled clients across all three investment channels – banks, independents and wire houses – yielded results that showed, in each channel, that the following attributes were valued more than returns:

1. An advisor's ability to explain complicated concepts easily.
2. How often the advisor checks in.
3. How completely the advisor manages expectations.

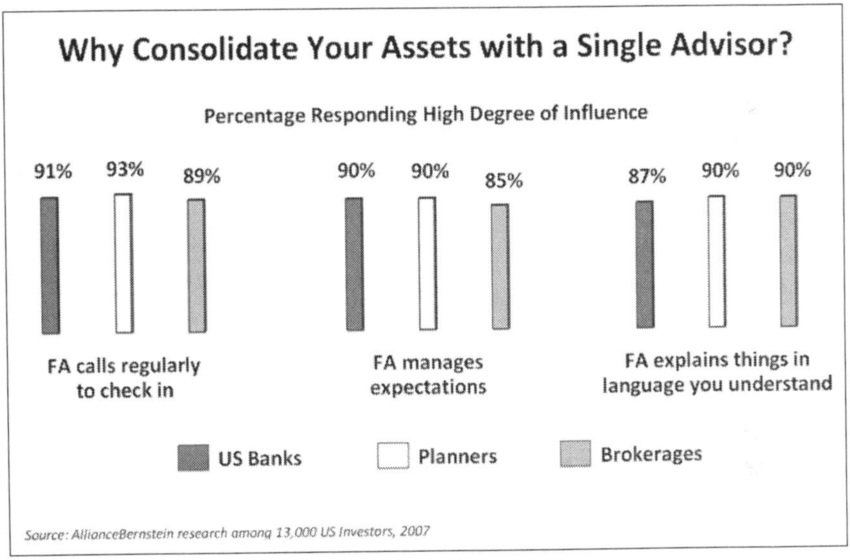

That all sounds fairly simple, doesn't it? You need to be easy to understand, call your clients more often and ensure that all your clients' expectations are met, which really means ensure that your clients know what your process is. Bonus points if they can remember it, and double bonus points if they can repeat it to someone else.

And yes, it's easy to do – once. But like absolutely anything new that you are trying to make a discipline, doing it consistently every day is a different story. It's not so easy is to do it every single time with every single client you have unless you rely on a set of processes that drive your client experience.

Investors are seeking to play a more active role in managing their portfolios by better understanding the markets. Advisors can set themselves up for success by engaging their clients in meaningful conversation and taking the time to explain the market forces at play. The key is that you manage their education. You are the interpreter and filter of all financial news.

Become an expert at being clear. Become a good listener. Empathize. Put yourself in your client's position as best you can. Ask clarifying questions: "Excuse me, David. I need to ask you something. A moment ago you said (this). I want to make sure I am clear what (this) means to you." Or you might say, "It's funny that you would mention that. I hear that from a lot of people who I meet. Tell me why it is important to you."

Sometimes when you are listening to your clients, do you ever find yourself wanting to stop them so that you can jump in with something to say that might help them? Sometimes that is appropriate. More often, however, you need to sit back and let them speak. You need to really hear the meta messages of what they are saying, those little meanings behind the words, so that you can respond accordingly. Let me give you an example that powerfully impressed upon me the attractiveness and value of good listening skills.

I was introduced to a sales manager named Jeff via a referral from a broker named Kevin who had just heard me speak. An email was sent to both Jeff and me suggesting we connect. I called Kevin to thank him, and he told me that Jeff was a fantastic person. Kevin felt very strongly that on a personal level, Jeff and I would click.

Jeff and I finally connected by phone, and within a minute it was clear to me that Jeff was in fact as advertised – a warm, easy person who truly listened to my words.

"Dennis, how are you?" he asked. I answered, "Fantastic." Now, this is the magic moment right here. He could have said, "Glad to hear it. Now what is it that Kevin thinks we need to talk about?" But he didn't. Instead he said, "Really? Tell me why you are fantastic." Ninety-nine out of a hundred people (or maybe more than one hundred people) would never have asked me that question. I know this. I do this for a living. I pay attention to these sorts of moments compulsively.

When someone is actually *listening* to you, and it's clear to you that they care about what you are saying, it is incredibly powerful. Especially when dealing with matters of trust.

So I shared my plans for the weekend with Jeff. I was going to spend Thanksgiving weekend at the cabin with my family. The leaves would be exploding with color, the fire would be on, and I'd muck around in the wood pile. He was quiet for a moment, and then he told me all about his cabin in the Adirondacks.

Of course, the stories soon drifted from general summertime fun reminiscences and wishes ("I'd like to be there right now") to more meaningful, legacy-related stories. We were now sharing with each other on the telephone the kind of people we really are, as human beings, not as positions.

Jeff isn't a sales manager for a Fortune 100 company, and I'm not the owner of a business looking to help him solve a problem. Or said another way, I wasn't sniffing around for understanding and opportunity.

Jeff and I shared this incredible connection. We both understood legacy and family, and because I felt that we were similar, I was more naturally inclined to trust him. And I still do. Jeff took an interest. He asked, and then nothing but goodness transpired.

Human beings love stories, and we especially love stories about us! We are hyper-communicators. We are plugged in because we like to be connected.

Stories are how we share the news and events of our days. We tell our friends about people at work, things we are working on, what he said, what she said, what they both couldn't say. Stories help us relate. We can empathize with the people we are hearing about because we relate it to a similar personal experience.

WIRED

I'm sure you are aware of the differences between left brain right brain thinking. VSAs rely on it; they know that people rationalize with the left side of their brain (facts, numbers, logic/reason) and are more intuitive and expressive with the right side (emotions, visualizing, empathy). When you only address financial facts, you are ignoring all the other factors that go into your clients' moods, feelings and judgments. That's not prudent.

Most of us don't think in numbers, we think in feelings. We don't remember the size of a number; we remember how the number made us feel. Your clients are going to think about how they feel in your presence. They will remember how they felt when they were with you, if they felt that you listened, that you understood. And from these feelings will arise the ultimate question: do I trust him?

Not only is it unwise to miss an opportunity for connection, but when you do, you risk sounding like every other advisor who is a data-dumper. When you do this, your business process doesn't necessarily reflect the process you use to select assets or build your portfolios. And it avoids completely what the experience of working with you is like.

Before you read any further, ask yourself what your current clients would tell you about what it's like to work with you. Would they be able to tell a friend or family member what happens in a year, how many face-to-face meetings they have with you, how many telephone calls? Would they be able to describe what it feels like to be your client and how they prepare for a meeting with you? Do they even feel prepared? Do they see each meeting as a stand-alone event, or do they see each meeting – indeed, each interaction with you – as a piece in a larger process?

Once again, think left brain/right brain. The most successful financial advisors, those who can afford to be selective about the clients they bring into their practice, are not merely technicians. While they know what they are talking about, they know more importantly how to talk about it. They appeal to the right brain sensibilities of their clients. As one advisor said to me, "You need to know about the money and also what the money is for." Your clients need to know that you and they are the heroes of their story.

You need to be an excellent communicator, illustrator and reporter. Without a doubt, you have to be able to clearly demonstrate that you are a professional. To put it candidly, your clients need to know that you possess the intellectual capacity to get this important job done.

Caring about your clients isn't a skill you can learn. If you are not interested in people, in helping them articulate their questions and helping them take steps to enrich themselves, then do yourself a favor and get a new job. You can, however, hone your skills so that you become better at understanding your clients, at empathizing with their needs. Most VSAs are curious about people and take the time to know them.

Clients very quickly come to weigh how easy you are to understand and how clearly you can explain your process. It's an intuitive decision on their part, and what they conclude can take place within the first five minutes of knowing you, or even faster. Malcolm Gladwell, in *Blink: the Power of Thinking Without Thinking*, writes that humans have learned – as a survival skill – to make snap decisions and judgments in as short a period as one or two seconds.[2] They evaluate every interaction with you, from the very first moment they hear your name to how they feel when they walk into your office. The wheels are constantly turning as they assess how good a job you will do at managing them. We may not even be conscious of some of these evaluations.

No detail, then, should be too insignificant for a successful advisor to consider. What you send along to a client before they meet with you, the steps you take to prepare them – each event is of critical importance.

FIRST DOWN, SECOND TO GO

Let's assume you are one of the lucky people who make connections easily. You enjoy and excel at casual conversation, and you are genuinely interested in other people. You fully comprehend that to be understood is a skill and a blessing. You agree that being able to clearly articulate your process is imperative, and furthermore, you agree that these two major considerations influence the experience for potential clients in determining how it would *feel* to be your client.

---

2 Malcolm Gladwell, *Blink: The Power of Thinking Without Thinking* (New York: Little, Brown and Company, 2005).

That is half the battle. The other half, consisting of the next three entrepreneurial attributes, is just as important.

1. A desire to do the work.
2. A desire to be the best version of oneself.
3. Self-discipline and accountability.

Let's explore this a little. A desire to do the work means a lot of things, but most importantly, it means that you finish. I don't want to be too metaphysical, but the moment you conceive of a PLAN B, you simultaneously create the reason for it. Most successful people don't have a PLAN B. Most successful people focus their energy on finishing PLAN A rather than on thinking up PLAN B. While a failing entrepreneur is sitting around thinking about how to stop, a successful entrepreneur is thinking about how to finish.

Know this: the vast majority of entrepreneurs have been brought to the point of failure, yet the experience only seals their success. You have to believe in what you are doing and you have to be willing to keep pushing it through, no matter the obstacles. Successful entrepreneurs aren't defeated by issues such as third-party contractors who are late or the lack of integration with back-office software. They just manage them better. They make mistakes, they learn from it, they adjust and it never happens again.

'Doing the work' means that VSAs are in charge, responsible, organized and don't waste their own time. They don't procrastinate nor do they kid themselves about what is involved. They are not plagued by bad habits.

Another thing I have noticed about VSAs is that they make more phone calls than not-so-successful financial advisors, who too easily dismiss the importance of professional phone habits in general, such as having a call schedule, returning calls. As a related observation, a successful sales manager once told me that he believes every person calls at least three people to get an answer to a question. When this manager was in sales, he would always strive to be the first or second person to answer when the call came in. That is his brand/experience and this is exactly what he now repeats over and over to his sales team.

Part of doing the work also means that VSAs keep very detailed notes. In the previous section, I mentioned that VSAs are process-oriented. Here's one thing that sets their processes apart: they are written down, measured and reviewed.

VSAs are disciplined overall, and they are inspired to be the very best people they can be, both professionally and personally. They are good spouses, good parents, good sons and daughters. Doesn't it just make sense that what you won't do for yourself personally you will not be able to do for yourself professionally? How on earth would you ever be able to wake up and focus on being "the best financial advisor" if you wake up feeling less than the best version of who you are as a person? So if that means dealing with some discomfort, facing the uglier sides of your personality, addressing and admitting your shortcomings, that's what it means. Figure out why and how you want to change them.

It has been proven that successful people also work on further developing their personal and professional skills. They are endless learners, full of curiosity, expanding their fund of knowledge whenever and wherever they can.

The life you are living, the circumstances you find yourself in, are not random. Your existence is a direct result of the questions you ask yourself. If you ask yourself, "How can I make my business grow?" the answer might be, "By bringing on more clients." There is nothing wrong with that question. Making more money can be a very good thing, as can enjoying your life to the fullest. You will get no argument from me there. But if you want to change your business, if you can't catch a break, maybe you need to change the questions you are asking.

Better questions will lead directly to better actions which lead to better results. So instead of asking, "How can I make my business grow?" instead ask, "What is it about what I do that people value the most? What kind of experience do I want to deliver to my clients? If I were a client, how would I want to be treated by this business?"

We know what it is that you do for a living, but even if you worked on a line assembling cars or making burgers, work to leave everything – people, places, communities – better than when you found them.

And finally, the big one: self-discipline and accountability.

Very successful people who are very successful advisors understand that you are nothing except what you repeatedly do. Your disciplines and your daily behavior are paramount. VSAs document processes, they figure out what is important and what works, and they do it the same way every single time.

VSAs know their performance metrics. They measure everything. And one of the things they measure is how they manage their energy because it is the most important factor of being able to manage tasks. To manage energy, you need clarity and a plan: clarity of purpose and a plan to get everything finished. Trying to get it all done by undertaking an unreasonable work load will not work – if anything, you will fall further behind.

The goal, then, is to build something that lasts, that is self-sufficient and that reflects the kind of excellence you bring to your person and your business. That takes implementing a process, but before you can do that, you have to first understand and initiate becoming the kind of person you need to be.

And in the next chapter, we'll look at that creature inside you who wants to keep that from happening.

RECAP

Very successful advisors (VSAs) are disciplined entrepreneurs whose practices stress processes and deliver engaging experiences to their clients. VSAs are driven by the desire – which they view as an obligation – to help others, not by personal gain. Their obligation manifests in creating alignment with clients and in ensuring the experience delivered to them is sincere.

Twenty percent of practice management should focus on financial matters. The remaining time should be devoted to developing and enhancing client relationships and experiences. The reason for this emphasis on relationship management is that studies show clients want clarity, regular communication and managed expectations from their advisor. Communicating clearly means appealing to both the emotional and logical needs of clients, listening carefully and responding in ways that are sincere, or authentic.

VSAs possess three core entrepreneurial traits: they consistently work hard, they strive to be the best versions of themselves, and they practice self-discipline and accountability. They are organized and in control, and they practice good business disciplines, such as taking careful notes, regularly contacting their clients and knowing their performance metrics.

Chapter 2

I Am the Lizard King

SO FAR SO GOOD, RIGHT? You've read the first chapter, and you are identifying with some of what you have read. You want to be the best version of yourself. You know that there is something special about how you see the world that makes you believe you can do this right, that you can accomplish your goals, live a life of virtue and find yourself in a big pile of *la dolce vita.*

Before I go any further, let me pay tribute to both Seth Godin and Steven Pressfield. These two men have had a tremendous personal influence on me and have contributed to my success professionally. It was Steven who first called resistance "the Lizard," and it was Seth who introduced me to Steven's writings. I have never met either man personally, but I hope one day to make that happen.

OLD CODE

I will formally give credit whenever I should, and in this case I have to acknowledge Ken Wood, my best friend and ski partner. Ken and I have spent hours discussing the concept of Old Code; I think he may have even coined the term. We will never know, and he will never care. Either way, a lot of my thinking and work – and therefore living – was influenced by those ski days.

Several years ago, Kenny and I started talking about ourselves, people in general, motivation and inspiration, fear, success, failure, desire and how all of it – all of this primal thinking – is driven by basic instinct. We started to refer to any kind of pre-programmed behavior or preference that we wanted to overcome as Old Code.

At the time, we were trying to master skiing through bumps and trees on the ski hill. What we found was that we had to learn how to see the pathways, rather than the tree trunks. Trust me, your instinct is telling you to not only look at the trees, but to appreciate that they are moving towards you. To succeed at our goal, we had to learn to think almost backwards. As a footnote to how well Ken and I undertook these lessons, Kenny courageously donated his lower right shin to this process and has 18 screws and some assorted parts to show for it.

Old Code shows up all over the place. Have you ever noticed that almost everyone is afraid of snakes and spiders? Nobody cares when they see an ant or a June bug or a Luna moth. But drop a spider in front of most people (myself included), and we are instantly repelled. Even writing about spiders is literally creeping me out.

Old Code is universal. As a species, we share the same evolution, and every human on the planet has the same processes running in the background. That's why so many people are afraid of spiders and snakes.

I have learned, then, that it is essential to a person's success that he or she truly understand and ultimately overcome their Old Code because it is largely becoming obsolete anyway. Not only that, but some aspects of it are actually harming us. I truly believe that we desire a transformation, that we know we need to create a New Code in order to gain insight, think differently and capitalize on opportunities.

CUE THE LIZARD

Old Code is very old and therefore very powerful. Old Code is real, and it lives in the oldest part of your brain – your Lizard brain – the part that has been around longer than our "upper mammalian brain," the one responsible for reason. The older the code, the more powerful it is, and the more difficult it is to overcome. Old Code loves you, and Old Code doesn't want to see you get hurt or miss out. Old Code wants to feed your basic human appetites, and Old Code wants to keep you safe – too safe.

Old Code keeps you from evolving and evaluating and adjusting.

Here is a good example: the stock market gets the stuffing taken out of it so that stocks of good companies are now really cheap or 'on sale,' as stock brokers like to say. But Old Code tells us not to buy them, to avoid them like a spider, don't lose any more money, flee to safety and basically "wait until it is once again expensive, then buy when it's safe." The newer part of your brain is trying to win with reasonable arguments, telling us what a bargain we could be getting, but Lizard brain is telling just the opposite, throwing any sense out the window. "Sell! Get out! Something left over is better than nothing left over!"

Old Code will make you hesitate when you should leap. Old Code will make you eat too much even though you desperately want to lose weight. Old Code will make you too cautious, believing you can't do something because you have not done it before.

For every one successful opportunity-seizing entrepreneur, there are scores of others with the same idea but whose Lizards are keeping them nice and safe. 'Nice and safe' is just another way of saying 'the status quo.'

I consider myself a successful entrepreneur. I have an enviable work/life balance. I work hard. In the past six months, I have flown more than seventy times to speak at conferences, and I have spent about three months living in different hotels. By the end of the year, I will have flown over one hundred times, for what will be about the twelfth year in a row. So I work a lot. And when I am on the road working, my days are often eighteen hours long. I'm not looking for sympathy. I just want to make sure you get the full picture.

But right now, as I write this, I'm up at the lake, sitting on the porch overlooking the water, typing while my little girls sleep away the early morning. Not surprisingly, everyone I know suddenly wants to be me.

The only reason they feel that way is because the option isn't there. They could all be me, but they would have to overcome *their* Old Code, and that is really difficult for them. Better to go to work and be told what to do than *risk* it all. Here's how I see it: the greater risk is living an ordinary life where one day, inevitably, you realize that everything should have been…more.

Stop giving your Old Code power. It is Old Code that stops you from calling a prospect whom you know you could help. Old Code tells you not to write your Series 7 exam and become a Financial Advisor, and it's Old Code that prevents you from calling a lawyer to discuss your $1,000,000 idea. Old Code is what tells you to settle and accept that this is the way it is, and that the way it is isn't so bad.

Had my mom thought that way, she never would have moved across the country at the age of seventeen to become a nurse. She never would have met my dad. Had my dad started to listen to his Old Code, he wouldn't have started his own business, and I never would have had for a father the man he became. I would have had some lookalike pretender as my role model, a person who worked for someone else and came home resenting his boss. What a horrible example that would have been.

Live (or die) by the rules you set. I say, "Get inspired." As Hunter S. Thompson once put it, "Buy the ticket, take the ride."

UNDERSTAND THE LIZARD

The Lizard is usually the most underrated opponent you ever face. As every fit person will tell you: exercising is easy, going to the gym is the hard part. That's the Lizard.

You can defeat the Lizard. You *will* defeat the Lizard. It takes time. It takes strategy. It takes faith and resilience because resistance is a given. Resistance is a constant, but it can and will be defeated.

Remember your intent. Remember that very successful people have a desire to be the very best version of themselves.

To understand resistance, you have to understand a little bit about how your brain works. As I mentioned earlier, the Lizard loves you. This is what makes the Lizard so difficult to defeat because he doesn't come at you like an adversary. He comes at you like an ambassador. The Lizard knows your innermost thoughts, hopes, fears and motivators. The Lizard knows you at your worst and best. The Lizard is also incredibly good at what he does. And that is to get you to accept the status quo, and convince yourself that the status quo is acceptable.

The Lizard doesn't make demands, he makes suggestions, and most of his suggestions make sense. They are easy little statements like, "Maybe you should wait. Sleep on it, and then see how you feel tomorrow." He simply suggests that maybe you are getting a little ahead of yourself, maybe you should slow down, read a book or two on the subject. Perhaps you should talk to some people, wait until next month, or next quarter, or even next year when circumstances might be better. The Lizard never says, "Absolutely not." The Lizard doesn't say, "You can't do it." He suggests that perhaps you shouldn't. With a long pause beforehand, he just says, "Wait."

Sooner or later, you will agree with him.

The reason the Lizard tells you to wait is because the Lizard wants you to be happy and safe. The Lizard doesn't want you to lose what you have, doesn't want you to jeopardize your health, your potential. The fear of losing what you have for anything less than certain is a risk, and the Lizard doesn't like risk. Risk is dangerous.

The Lizard just wants to rationalize your lack of action. And sometimes, the Lizard isn't even thinking about keeping you safe and healthy. Just try to quit smoking to hear what he has to say about that. "Hey, I love you man, and I want you to quit smoking too. However, there are 25 cigarettes in a package, so you may as well smoke the last eleven. What the heck, savor them while you're at it. After all, they will be your very last ones."

Except Monday on your way to work, you buy another packet.

The easiest thing in the world is to start something, and the hardest thing in the world is to finish it and make it permanent.

Do you have any idea how long I have been working on this book? So long that once I see it completed, cover to cover, I sometimes think I won't be proud of it. I fear that I will think that all the time and money wasn't really worth it – that I should somehow have more, that I let myself down. Because of this, I feel that when I am done, if this book is anything less than one thousand pages and riding high on the *New York Times* best seller list, it will ultimately have been a failure. Maybe I should just stop.

The Lizard doesn't want me to write the book. If I write the book, you might like it, and then you might call me or pass the book along to someone you know. And then someone might ask me to do something, like speak at a conference. They might ask me to speak about something I'm not completely comfortable talking about. So then I might have to do some research on the subject so that I feel confident enough to lecture on it. And on it goes.

The truth is that you and I slay the Lizard with self-discovery.

Personal growth happens when you face something you are uncomfortable with or find challenging, and then you deal with it. Part of that process may involve understanding why you didn't like it in the first place. Ergo, if I write the book, good things might happen. If good things happen, I might have to become more of a person, a better version of myself. This is a scary proposition for The Lizard. I might have to upgrade my software, slap in a memory card or – to hell with it – just switch to a Mac.

When you start thinking about how great anything can be once you make a change, you have to deal with resistance. So with that considered, I encourage you to read this book with the mindset of a finisher. This book isn't about starting as much as it's about finishing.

When you – and by extension, your enterprise – are built around the principle of finishing, it becomes an obligation. You build your practice around this obligation.

Just know that the Lizard will rile against this. The closer you get to doing it, the stronger the resistance. When you start to get smarter, when big pieces start to click, when you see all the pieces and steps begin to line up and for the briefest of most wonderful moments, your dream becomes real, just know that those moments are like swords into the Lizard. And understandably, he will react. Violently.

SLAYING THE LIZARD AND MAKING SHIFT HAPPEN

You may want to have something to write in – don't let the Lizard tell you that you should buy a more appropriate book. Just grab something that works, and write it down. You can transcribe it later.

There is a magic recipe for defeating the Lizard and improving your life in three steps:

1. Expect more of yourself.
2. Redefine what you think is possible for yourself.
3. Re-evaluate your strategy, and when necessary, change it.

Expect more of yourself.

When you raise your expectations for and of yourself, you change not only what you believe is personally possible but also what is personally acceptable.

All of those nagging things that you don't like about yourself that you wish you could change? These negative influences and feelings rob you of faith and energy. Being at odds with yourself causes you to focus your energy inside instead of outside, where it needs to be.

You are containing or controlling instead of designing and soaring.

When I first sat down to try this exercise on my own, to write out what I expected for myself, I wrote that I wanted to own my own company. I wrote that I wanted to be important and indispensable to my clients. I wanted to be respected, and I wanted not only my opinion but my effort to be appreciated. I wanted to be introduced by my clients as someone who changed their lives. I wrote that I wanted to be a catalyst for change and I wanted to be a leader.

I also wrote down that I wanted to be married, have a family, live in a nice house, go on vacations, drive nice cars and not worry about my cash flow. I wanted to save money, be on top of things, and eventually retire.

I won't bore you with the rest of it. It's likely that my list was very similar to yours. So now it's your turn. Write your list. I'll wait.

Next, make a list of all the things about yourself that you find truly unacceptable. We all have a list, and we all have big things and little things on it. It's your list and it's private. Just write it down. Some of the things you will put on your list might not seem so terrible or serious – but they are all important.

One of the most important adjustments I made in my life seemed pretty simple at the time and yet facing it and fixing it has been incredibly profound. Truly, by making this one single shift, I have made hundreds of thousands of dollars.

I wrote down that being tired was personally unacceptable. I hate feeling tired. When I am tired, my brain feels like it has mud on it. Nothing fires right. There are no connections, no spark, no insight, no…me. In almost every case, when I am tired, I miss out on opportunity. It literally costs me a lot of money. Not only that, but when I am tired I can be a jerk. I can say insensitive or, at best, not helpful things to hotel staff or people in general, and I hate it when I feel like I need to go back and apologize for being mean.

I accepted that any time I was tired, I had failed.

I couldn't deliver the Dennis Experience when I was tired. If I was tired, I couldn't get up early, fuel myself properly and then tackle my day with purpose and awareness. When I was tired – when I *am* tired – I don't eat at the right time, which leads me to make horrible food choices, which then leads to me being a big fat mammal who is not only tired but also unhappy and full of internalized anger and disappointment. Imagine what I'm like after a few days in a row of being tired. Now imagine someone calls and wants to speak with me about an opportunity, and my assistant asks me if I can speak to this person on Friday. After a few days of being tired, I'm far more interested in my own self than I am in learning about someone else's problems. Just by being tired, I fail to be who I am and I fail to fulfill my obligation.

See how all this can spiral out of control just because I am a little sleepy? Consider the lost opportunity.

Life is hard enough. I have to be able to at least count on having 'me' on my own side. So getting enough rest and making the adjustment in my behavior paid off instantly, and it continues to pay dividends.

Get your list going, and don't allow the Lizard to tell you what you can't do. We'll get to him.

Adjust what you think is possible for yourself.

How on earth are you going to successfully raise your own personal expectations if you don't believe it's possible? You are going to sabotage yourself before you even get started. Only when you believe in yourself can you dig deep. When your inner voice is telling you it can't be done, you may as well put the load down and quit.

When required, change your strategy.

When you are not getting the results you desire, you are obligated to re-evaluate your strategy. When it's not working, it's not working. Something needs to change, and resisting this change isn't going to get you anywhere.

I have said this before, and I will say it again: one of my greatest weapons is my ability to drop an idea of mine that I love for someone else's idea that I recognize is better than mine. I waste virtually no time or money protecting my ego.

When you have people who work with you or for you, then it's in your own self-interest to ensure that they feel as encouraged as possible to offer up some ideas. The worst thing that can happen to your enterprise is having people sitting on their suggestions. In my company, I want everyone involved to feel they can contribute and that what they say matters to me.

What is your current strategy? What is working? What isn't?

So we've covered how you can begin to achieve a quantum shift in your life and business. You now expect more of yourself, have a higher opinion of what you believe you are capable of, and you are embracing change and re-evaluating your strategy.

The next step is crucial. Ready?

Quit lying to yourself.

How long have you been kicking around the notion of change? What kind of stall tactics has the Lizard introduced to your behavior to stop you from committing?

Sometimes the act of evaluation – of pondering, considering, or discussing – is actually dangerous. It might make you feel better, but it's a placebo. It is not change.

Only action will lead to achievement. Everything else is simply engaging in wool gathering, or as my wife likes to say, "Talking to the band."

Stop talking to the band. Instead, start playing your song. Your song is why you are here. Failing to face and fix your problems by deluding yourself is personally treasonous. You are telling yourself, in the voice of the Lizard, that you are not worth the effort. Surely that has to hurt. If you don't believe in yourself, nobody else will. They will just be following your lead.

To make this shift happen, you have to start to understand *why* you want to make this change, not *how* to make it. When the *why* is clear, the *how* will follow.

How does this next word make you feel?

Satisfaction.

I want you to imagine that you have engaged in some personal growth, faced your demons, called yourself on your nonsense, committed to change, committed to better habits, and suddenly your income has quadrupled. Now I want you to imagine that whatever changes you made have been lasting. You have ushered in change and process and predictability, so much so that your new income is now your old income.

The root of all evil is not money. The root of all evil is instant gratification. Just because you like it doesn't mean it's good for you. Just because it makes you happy doesn't mean it's good for you. Whoever said, "If it feels good, do it" was an idiot. Tell that to a crack addict. Tell that to an alcoholic. Tell that to a person who has no personal integrity.

What do you think is going to give you the most satisfaction? The money? Or something else, something better, something more noble?

What will bring you the most satisfaction, long lasting, deeply fulfilling, is not the income but rather the feeling you will have when you look at what you have created. Something better, more lasting. Something that has, perhaps, enriched the lives of others. Something real.

A few years ago while I was on a flight, I had a conversation with a personal trainer. He gave me a simple tip, but first he allowed me to blabber on for about thirty minutes about all the challenges I was having just to maintain a healthy weight.

After I let it all out, it was his turn. He gave me a simple, brief suggestion. He told me it would change my life if I embraced it.

He told me to go to bed earlier.

He didn't talk about diets, avoiding carbs or working out. His argument was that if I went to bed earlier, I'd get up earlier, have more time and would be able to eat breakfast, which he suggested should be oatmeal and fresh fruits. He explained that eating right away would jump start my metabolism, and that by not eating, I was telling my body to starve, not start, not burn fat. It sounded perfectly logical to me.

He then added that when lunch came around, I would likely not be hungry and that I must (not should) eat anyway. He told me that since I wouldn't be hungry, I wouldn't really care what I was eating, and I should eat a nice lo-cal turkey sandwich. He told me that at dinner, I likely wouldn't be hungry either but that I should eat anyway. "Never get hungry," he said. "When you are hungry, you will have no self discipline. You will give into *desire*."

To desire is to lose.

When I don't go to bed early, I break all the rules. I give in to impulse. I order room service. I eat like I am on my way to the electric chair. The Lizard offers all kinds of convenient points to help me rationalize. "Order the medium pizza to your room and eat it in your underwear. Make sure when you answer the door you are wearing pants. Then take them off and eat an entire pizza, alone. It's not that bad; you have not eaten all day."

When I do what I need to do, what I must do, I obey all the rules, the rules I want to follow, and at the end of the day I am satisfied. A deep-rooted satisfaction. So much so that it may not be satisfaction I am experiencing at all. It may, in fact, be *pride*. There is nothing wrong with being proud of oneself.

So do you want to change and achieve a life less ordinary? Do you want to be the very best version of yourself, to overcome the Lizard?

Then get moving. Quit lying. Don't consider. Don't evaluate. Don't take some time. Start.

Start by stopping. Stop lying. Stop telling yourself it can't be done. Expect more and be more.

You can do this.

DEEP SHIFT

Perhaps you have seen me speak a few times and you keep coming to hear me. Are you waiting for me to say something else? Something to get you moving? It's not me. It's you.

Well, more specifically, it's your Lizard. He has you believing that just listening to me or reading this book is going to help. It's not helping. It's masking. It's making you feel good.

I know it may not seem like much of a strategy, but frankly, "Give 'er" is possibly the best strategy I have ever heard.

Your Lizard will become especially active when you engage in any activity or pursuit that rejects instant gratification for a goal more noble, fulfilling and meaningful to you. The Lizard will show up on amphetamines if you are attempting anything that is really important to you, which you have failed to succeed at previously. This could be artistic pursuit, an entrepreneurial endeavor, higher education, personal improvement or perseverance in many forms, including but certainly not limited to skiing really steep beautiful mountains covered with trees and moguls.

Let's return for a moment to my skiing analogy. When you slay the Lizard, the moguls and trees are known as 'features.' and each run is full of infinite possibility – a wonderful metaphor for life, really. When The Lizard is gnawing on you, moguls and trees are known as 'dangerous' and you risk missing out on the wild woods, the rare air. You miss the invitation to join the howling Dirt Bags, those who eat their bagged and beaten lunch on the chair lift, carry their own water and suck the marrow out of life. You know who you are, and I salute you.

It's a matter of opinion, but I think you risk missing everything.

Life is never better. Life is now, and the clock is ticking. We are all dead. The question is when, and what you will do from now until then?

David Gerrold, writing as his alter ego Solomon Short, once said: "As soon as you rationalize, you are wrong."

You know that somewhere inside of you there is someone else – another you, if you will – who wants more and is waiting for the other you to figure it out so that you can move onward and upward to a better place, a better you.

So here is what you need to do. Think like a little kid.

Kids don't so much think as *know* that anything and everything is possible. Kids and crazy people think anything is possible, but you and I wrestle with that truth. We know it all, yet we believe nothing.

Don't think. Act. Move. Go. Do. Start. Begin. Continue. Embark. Commit.

If you can't think of committing to your job or your talent or your passion, then get out of it and find what you can commit to. You might be barking up the wrong tree. Focus. Keep negative people and negativity at bay. Share a deep secret. You can't get forward focusing in. Whatever it takes, do it.

Don't fret. Don't think, analyze, wait or reason.

The worst thing that will happen is you will flame out and fail miserably. So what? It's not the first time. I'd rather die trying then live lying.

I talked earlier in Chapter One about how successful people typically live lives of virtue and principle. I examined the fact that they like to do things as much as the rest of us but that they have discipline, a vision, a plan. They measure their results, and they do not trade long-term profit for short term reward. They stand over their slain lizards with a chest thump. They stick to their plans, they believe in their processes, and they work towards them. They give 'er.

Now that you are ready to do so as well, you need to have a path to walk down. It's time to plan your strategy.

RECAP

The Lizard is our brain's 'Old Code,' our resistance to any change that involves risk or disturbing the status quo. The Lizard is defeated when we build New Code and expect more of ourselves, redefine our possibilities and re-evaluate our strategy for change. The first step in defeating the Lizard is to...*take* the first step.

Chapter 3

The Shift: What You Think You Know About Strategy, Value Propositions and Alignment

EVERYTHING YOU HAVE READ so far about the characteristics of VSAs and the resistance to change they constantly strive to overcome could be regarded as a the equivalent of preparing a work site: leveling the ground, clearing away debris, shoring up the earth. Your business is the beautifully designed and executed structure that will arise from it. And the first thing that needs to happen, now that the site has been prepared, is to lay a solid, long-lasting foundation that will be constructed of strategy, value proposition and alignment.

Your **strategy** is your reason for being. Your **value proposition** is the experience you promise to each and every client. **Alignment** is ensuring that what you deliver to your clients fulfills both what they desire and what you promised. When all of these objectives are met, and your services consistently deliver a set of experiences that are predictable, well-executed and anticipated, then you have created your unique **brand.**

In other words, ensuring you have a sound foundation is essential to your success because it forms the way you look at the world. The underlying principle and purpose of the foundation is to ensure that the purpose of your business and what your audience wants are aligned and that you share a common sense of purpose.

In the first chapter, I wrote that your obligation was to deliver a superior client experience. That's the top floor. So how do we get there?

A TALE OF STRATEGIC REALIGNMENT

You have had some fun reading about the type of person a VSA is, and you have gained a little more insight into the Lizard.

From a practical point of view, we've looked`at how to defeat it. Now we'll learn how to do it tactically. You need two things. First, you need a deep insight and understanding of the problem, challenges, opportunities and realities of your situation. Secondly, you need a plan that delivers the solutions to your enterprise's obstacles, one that manages your resources, time, energy and money.

What you need at this juncture is a shift. You need to re-evaluate your strategy and ensure that the experience you provide the ideal type of client you choose to work with is aligned with the experience that people like that are looking for. To accomplish this, a shift in your strategy may be required.

Let's look at a case study. IBM is an excellent example of a company that shifted strategies. IBM started out by creating cash registers, which were themselves a solution to a problem – making it easier to keep paper records of transactions. As time wore on, IBM moved to selling typewriters and then computers. It was a natural progression, as all of these products fit the corporate strategy of providing solutions.

Then IBM lost its way. It got sucked into becoming a product company, and it thought of itself less and less as a solutions company. Its strategy had changed; its reason for being, its purpose, its passion, its obligation were no longer in finding and providing solutions for businesses, but rather in selling products.

By the mid to late 1980s, IBM was a mess. It was completely off course, selling all kinds of office machines that included computers with their own operating systems, a strategy which put it into direct competition with Microsoft.

Eventually, Dell crushed the PC market, Microsoft took over the software market, and IBM started shaking in its boots. It had never intended to be in the product business, solutions had always been its *raison d'être*, yet here it was. It was now staring at a plan no longer aligned with its customers' expectations.

So what did it do? It SHIFTED. It threw the old out, kicked the status quo to the curb and ushered in a new order! It fired its CEO, bought Lotus and got back to focusing on being what it was meant to be, a solutions company. It sold off the computer division to China in the early 2000s (it's Lenovo now), and it rebranded itself.

IBM Solutions. IBM e-business. IBM e-commerce.

In the past year, its stock has topped $200 on the NYSE, and as I type, fifty-six percent of their revenue comes from outside North America. IBM is now a global solutions provider. Its new initiative and message is 'Smarter Planet.' IBM is a company that innovates around using technology to make the planet smarter, easier, more efficient and more effective at solving problems. Talk about a serious shift.

Out with the blue suits, in with the new guys who want to roll up their sleeves and solve problems! Can I hear an 'amen'?

YOU ARE ABOUT TO STEP IN A LITTLE SHIFT

As industries mature and evolve, so do their clients. Consumers need change. Their awareness and understanding of the goods and services they are looking for changes, and the competition for their business increases. Costs come down as more products and players enter the game.

In the 1980s, financial advisors competed on product – who had what, and who had more of it. Investors needed investments, and they placed value – or perceived value – on whoever had the best products, the most products, and the best returns.

Then investors became a little smarter. They were more informed. Financial information in the form of books, magazines, newspaper articles, the Internet, cable news networks and radio flooded the market, and value shifted to information and knowledge.

The result was that, in essence, the industry began to concede to its clients that at the end of the day, it wasn't about the products but about the application. Advisors were getting on board with the idea that what consumers were paying for was their expertise. I started working in this industry in 1996, and at that time, one of the ways that advisors were growing their businesses was to pay financial speakers to come in and talk about compound interest and mutual funds. At the end of these events, which were packed, advisors would book appointments like crazy. I won't mention names, but back then there was one fellow in Canada who was a lock. Book him, people would show up, he'd sell them, and an advisor would be swamped with appointments.

I also remember when all of that stopped. It was a cliff. All of a sudden, people didn't want information anymore. This aforementioned nameless speaker was never heard from again. Suddenly, the luncheons and evening seminars that had been buzzing with potential business were empty. Crickets.

Value had shifted again. The client might as well have been saying, "You all have the same products, and you all say that you have the inside information. But now, due in large part to the Internet, I feel I have the same information. There are sixty-seven million (roughly) television programs and websites devoted to money, the markets, investing, insight, you name it. I can have access to it in six seconds dot com. Not only that, I can buy and sell online all by myself. I don't need a broker. I can be my own broker."

And as they came to learn, a little information can be a dangerous thing. The influx of self-investors coincided with the market correction surrounding the tech bubble. A lot of novice investors took a beating, which savvy advisors were able to capitalize on by underscoring that nothing could replace professional expertise and prudence.

After this, advisors sought to lure investors back with the next solution, fee-based investing. Take *that*, inevitable evolution of the financial services industry!

Now the message was: we'll do it all for 1.5% or thereabouts. No more commissions. The business had shifted away from sales and into a more consultative approach. There was less of an emphasis on products and returns and educational infotainment. Investors had access to new fee-based platforms, and there was a new trend towards a holistic approach to financial planning.

Now the shift was to lifestyle planning and retirement as boomers ripened a little more. With the growth phase of their portfolios now behind them, boomers' preoccupation became – and is – having a plan that provides income. They have the money, they want it to last, and they want to learn about how they can enjoy it.

More advisors today host non-financial events for clients than at any other time. I personally meet thousands of advisors in a year and shake a lot of hands. I have many conversations, and I know first-hand that we are here again. We are set for a change. We need to make some shift happen.

YOU BETTER START SWIMMING OR YOU'LL SINK LIKE A STONE, FOR THE TIMES THEY ARE A-CHANGIN'

Whether you realize it or not, we have already shifted to an experience economy, and for the first time the consumer is telling us what is needed. Up until this point, we have been dictating to them: you need products, you need specific advice. You need information and content. You need a bundled solution at a comparable and competitive rate.

But as we've seen, they are telling you what they need. They need you to be easy to understand. They need to know your process. And they need to get a sense that you are enjoyable to work with. Investors want a leader.

They now accept that there is so much information, so many products and competing opinions that what they need now is someone whom they can follow. They want someone they understand, someone they can trust to navigate them through this minefield of options.

They are looking for you. They need you to lead them.

I hope you felt the slightest shift there. Just a little tug, but not yet the whole enchilada.

We have made it all the way to Chapter 3 before I have felt the need to use a hockey metaphor. That is rather impressive when you consider that I am Canadian and that I love the game. I am going to reference the incomparable Wayne Gretzky, who said, "A good hockey player plays where the puck is. A great hockey player plays where the puck is going to be."[3]

Let me extrapolate on what The Great One was saying: don't get there late. When you are watching it happen, you might as well be in the stands. Learn to watch what *is* happening, and become the next part of it.

When you get there late, you can still be a decent producer, but you miss the opportunity to be amazing. To be a hero, to be fantastic and awe-inspiring. You miss the opportunity to be the best version of yourself. You miss everything. Think of Apple and the iPhone compared to everyone else.

That cynicism you might have just felt? That's the Lizard messing with ya.

Where is the financial services industry headed? What do your clients want and value, and how will that change in the years ahead? Don't get lost in that last question. Just think about it from a general perspective. What do they need now? What will they need later? What business are you in?

This is why this chapter is titled *The Shift* because most people don't really think about their business as a living organism. They are playing catch up. I'm willing to bet that most independently-owned enterprises and entrepreneurs don't really fully understand what business they are in.

Are you still selling products? Are you telling people what they value? Are you competing on complete financial planning at a convenient fee?

As I mentioned earlier, your strategy is your reason for being. You can't know this until you first know what business you are in, and what you are going to offer and to whom. Strategy is your purpose. It's your obsession. Fulfilling your strategy is why you get up every day.

"We change people's lives."

---

[3] Wayne Gretzky, Rick Reilly, *Gretzky: An Autobiography* (New York: HarperCollins, 2001).

"I am a wicked sales machine!"

"To give every student in my class some attention!"

"To deliver peace of mind!"

"To be the best dad I can be!"

"To inspire people to innovate and accelerate meaningful change in their lives and businesses!"

This is really important because what your business should be built around is fulfilling your reason for being. I cannot stress more the importance of this premise.

If a fast food restaurant has a strategy to "sell a lot of grab-and-go food that tastes good to the customers," then everything the restaurant puts into its plan is going to be measured against this strategy. So when the restaurant owners ask themselves, "Does putting in a drive-through window help us sell more food that tastes good to customers?" and the answer is, "Yes, it does" then presto: drive-through windows are the norm.

Do you remember when the McDonald's fast food chain briefly experimented with pizza? It didn't last long. How come? Because as a plan it was not aligned with the needs of their clients, nor was it aligned with McDonald's strategy.

McDonald's strategy, one that they have mastered, is to sell a lot of food that tastes good to its customers quickly. Pizza wasn't fast enough. All of a sudden, their clients were confronted with a new experience at McDonald's.

Waiting.

There are a sufficient number of restaurants in which waiting is the norm, and that is a different experience altogether. Can you see how McDonald's could make the mistake though? From their perspective, they were already crushing the burger business. As far as burgers went, they were mindful of industry trends and of the new players on the block, and they remained vigilant to protect that profit stream.

However, McDonald's determined that an awful lot of money was being spent every year on pizza. They projected that figure into the future, figured out the big profit margins, falsely determined that it was a natural line extension and then, a kabillion dollars later and a whole lot of pizza on their face, they backed out.

Why? Because they figured it out. Their purpose is not to sell food that humans think is delicious, but rather to deliver an eating experience that is consistent and predictable. Therefore, as much as it looked like a natural fit and a good idea, selling pizza was actually a bad idea that was inconsistent or not aligned with the McDonald's experience. You don't go to McDonald's to wait; you go to McDonald's to get what you want in less than two minutes and never be surprised by what it is.

Shifting? Even a little?

Let's assume that you have it right, and the advisor sitting beside you reading the same book has it wrong.

His strategy, why he gets out of bed every day, is "to beat the S&P 500 and be in the top 10% quartile for advisor returns!" He has determined that the things that are going to differentiate him from the competition are his superior returns.

That is a perfectly fantastic strategy providing he is working for people who want that. This is often a good strategy when your clients are institutions, for example, or pension plans.

According to literally every single study ever done on what investors value, we can conclude with certainty that individual investors do not place as much of an emphasis on returns as we assume they do.

I'm not arguing that investors are unhappy with superior returns. What I am saying is that they do not value them; they expect them. In actual fact, the financial benchmark that investors are most concerned with is the one they have to achieve according to their *own* plan. They could care less about how their performance measures up against other investments or indices. They only care about hitting the targets dictated by their plan.

Think about what your fellow reader with the bad strategy does all day – what does his plan look like? He thinks he sells better performance, so every aspect of his plan would be aligned to achieve this goal. I bet he would send out a lot of performance information. He'd spend a lot of time studying charts, listening to conference calls, doing research and building portfolios. Everything he did would be focused on fulfilling his promise and obligation to generate superior financial returns. When he hosts events for his clients, I would imagine they would be technical in nature, and if a speaker were featured, it would be someone who speaks about finances, economics and/or investing.

This approach would align with the business he assumes he is in.

To use a metaphor, his strategy and plan are a radio station, and he is just off-station. His music is coming in a little fuzzy. It's getting the job done and it's catching some listeners, but too many of them are tuning in somewhere else. Or they soon will be when they hear something more to their liking. Our advisor friend thinks he is in a business he isn't actually in. He has no idea.

THE VALUE PROPOSITION AS AN OBLIGATION

Now we need to consider the next step. Once you know your strategy, you can develop your value proposition, which is your promise of what the client receives when they invest with you. The value proposition is the specific promise you make, but it often delivers something far more profound to the client.

For a moment, I want to explore the notion of the value proposition – your promise – and the idea of obligation.

You may like your job for reasons such as the opportunity for financial reward and the relative freedom of running your own practice. However, these reasons may not have been enough to have allowed you to feel passionate about what you do. Earlier, when we uncovered some of the attributes which distinguish entrepreneurs from ordinary business owners, we touched on the factor of passion. And passion starts when you identify your strategy and love fulfilling it. I want you to consider your work as your art. Being a fantastic financial advisor is your craft, not your job. It's who you are. Being a financial advisor and being in the service of others, helping them achieve their best version of themselves, is a noble and perfect calling.

Fast food restaurants promise food that people think tastes good, but these restaurants also deliver a consistent and reliable experience that is, to some degree, comforting.

The analogy is also pertinent to your practice, as I've been illustrating. You provide many services: a plan, insight, proposals, solutions, implementation and eventual financial independence. What your clients receive, however, is peace of mind and security. What you promise is to be a professional, but what you actually deliver is entirely different when you measure the emotional aspect of your client relationships.

Do you accept this? I hope you do because this is what people are paying you for. Otherwise, everyone would go to an online investment provider.

Give yourself some credit for why your clients chose you. You are amazing! Do you think they come to you only to hear about performance? That's obviously part of it, but do you think they get no value, or next to no value, from the rest of your relationship? Come on. They have bought into your passion.

As I mentioned in the last chapter, what they are looking for – what they need – is for you to be a leader. So lead them.

Redefine your strategy. Redefine your value proposition and then make this promise your obligation. I will use myself as an example.

What does my company, Dennis Moseley-Williams Strategic Consulting (or DMWSC since I have more than enough names) do? The apparent answer is that we provide business development solutions to the financial services industry on a corporate and individual level.

The reality? We inspire financial advisors to innovate and accelerate meaningful change in their lives and their businesses.

Conclusion? DMWSC is a company that innovates around the idea that clarity of purpose and process will lead to a better business through engineering a perfect client experience.

The business plan that I follow is built to ensure that I fulfill my promise – to inspire people to innovate and change. However, if I thought I were in the selling solutions business, I'd be on the phone all day trying to sell stuff. I'd have another person on the phone mining my database. I'd be selling CDs, DVDs and all kinds of product. That's not the business I am in. That's not what my clan wants.

Because I am clear on my strategy (purpose) and my promise (obligation), I have managed to align my plan to fulfill the specific needs and preferences of my clients. As a result, I am on target. I am effective. I can measure it. I can adjust the positioning of my services so that my delivery matches it to ensure a strategic fit with my clients' needs and expectations.

Your strategy leads to your promise which in turn forms your plan. And your plan then consistently delivers the desired experience of your clients.

Your obligation is your brand.

Are you shifting a little? Are you thinking about your plan now, how formal it is and how it is built with purpose? Or are you wondering, "What does a plan taste like?"

I hate to get all positive and motivational on you, but let me anyway. It's entirely possible that you are very close to a major breakthrough. Your clients like you, but they may not yet love you. They respect you, but they may not yet trust you. They work with you, but they may not yet empower you. They like you enough, but they don't refer even though most financial advisors cite 'increasing referrals' as a critical business goal. You know you are close, but you're just not there yet.

We are going to dig into plans, managing resources and setting up an official experience matrix later in the book. For now, let's carve out a little bit more of an understanding on plans, alignment experiences and brands.

Your plan is how you will leverage your available resources to deliver your promise. In your case, it will involve onboarding clients, rebooting existing relationships, review meetings, calls, networking meetings and all manner of other things unique to your practice.

The plan is your strategy in motion. If your strategy is to ultimately establish trust with your clients through an exceptional and consistent commitment to a delightful client experience, then the plan is how you will do it. For example, will having an amazing front-line person managing your inbound communication be part of your overall strategy? The plan is the CRM you will need, obtain and set up so that your front-line person can effectively fulfill your obligation. The plan is the meeting where you sit down and explain your wishes and expectations to your clients and their referrals. The plan is the script.

Your plan delivers your corporate Experience. And what is your Experience? Your Experience is your reason for being, your obsession, what you and your team rally around.

There is a better word for this. Brand. Most people think a brand is a logo. It is not. The experience you provide to clients and prospective clients is your brand. And a brand is one of two things. It is either a promise kept or a promise broken. That's it. Your brand is your emotional connection to your clients. It's not only your promise fulfilled, but also what you represent to your clients.

When your strategy is off, your promise is wrong, your obligation is pointless and your plan is ineffective. You are out of *alignment*. All the while, you are striving to be indispensable and critical to the lives of your clients, but you are not meeting their basic needs.

To deliver what I refer to as a finely-tuned Experience Factor, you will need to rely on strategy and proper value proposition so that they align with your existing and desired client needs and values. Supporting these efforts will be a plan which serves as the method to evolve and innovate in your business so that you are able to accelerate in the business environment you are in.

These tools – in this case, processes and protocols – will harness your time, energy and money towards a defined outcome.

RECAP

Strategy can be defined as understanding what you really do so that you can align the experience your business delivers with the desired experience of your clients. In other words, strategy is about providing a consistent match (or strategic fit) between your positioning and your delivery.

Positioning refers to how your company is seen from the outside. It includes how your customers will perceive you (and by association themselves); how your competitors will see your company; and how your company reacts and responds to all external stakeholders.

Delivery describes what your business is really good at, and the special skills, tools, or services it provides clients that enable you to solve their problems better than your competitors.

Achieving a perfect strategic fit by implementing the best strategies available allows you to be proactive in what you do and consistent in your results.

The competitive forces that drive innovation in the financial service industry have changed in the past three decades and have broadened their focus. Whereas the focus was on products in the 1980s and knowledge in the 1990s, the following decade saw a clear shift to the uniqueness of client experiences. This move toward experience is consistent with the general backdrop of a consumer environment that focuses on experience as a competitive differentiator.

In the present business environment, successful advisors will ensure that they understand the business they are really in. They will implement a value offering that ensures the client experience is aligned with their business strategy. The question then becomes: are all the activities that go on in your practice focused on the outcomes you are looking to create for your clients? If they are not, you run the risk of degrading the overall impact of how your clients perceive you. A well-aligned business will not only consistently meet and exceed existing client expectations, but it will be attractive to those who are not yet clients. This strategy will ensure that you have the foundation in place to build a business that will be profitable, effective and efficient for years to come.

Chapter 4

Managing Time, Energy and Money

YOU ARE SHIFTING NICELY, and your strategy is now hashed out, your promise reborn. This promise – the experience you will deliver – is now your obligation.

Every business in the world has three main resources that it uses to fulfill its promise. These resources are time, energy and money.

When your business is functioning properly with a clear strategy, and when the strategic plan (the tactics) is aligned, the business is in balance. Managing your three resources is almost effortless.

Most advisors mismanage their resources for two critical reasons.

1. **They have no idea how much time it takes them to manage their practice, nor do they even know how much time they have available in any given year.** These advisors work hard all the time, but they have no real way of knowing how they are doing. With the best of intentions, they believe that if they work hard all the time, they will get everything done. In general, they spend too much time with the wrong clients.
2. **They don't run their business with an entrepreneurial workweek in place.** Instead they rely on a bureaucratic workweek which

typically means a nine to five workday spanning Monday to Friday. They rely little on process or strategic planning, and they tend to work on whatever is in front of them. The irony is that they fall further behind, and they never get to the most important and powerful activities.

CLIENT SEGMENTATION AND BASIC SERVICE REQUIREMENTS

You may be tempted to skip this part, but please don't. You may think you know everything you either need to know or that there is to know about client segmentation, and the desire to skim might be tempting. But read it anyway. If you don't, you will miss an essential understanding of what you need to do, and you stand to jeopardize everything that follows.

Client Segmentation is all about gaining control over what truly drives your business: your clients and your management of time. Client Segmentation is the framework that focuses your business on identifying the right client for the right reasons, and in aligning those clients with your value proposition.

If you accept that not all clients are created equally, then you must conclude that the value proposition of your business will align and resonate with a certain type of person and not necessarily another. This is perfectly understandable.

The decisions you make about how you segment your clients will ultimately affect the short, mid and long-term outcomes of your business. As an advisor, you must believe that you have a choice regarding who you work with. Our objective at this point is to hash out a basic understanding of the time you require to service your clients and then, who your ideal clients might be.

An important benefit of the Client Segmentation process is to identify the attributes and characteristics of the type of clients who will be the most receptive to the experience you provide through your Experience Matrix, which is just another term for the hub of experiences you intend to provide your clients. In addition, Client Segmentation creates a dynamic for the growth of your business, providing a common framework for all team members to know exactly the value that any given client brings to the business.

For the point of illustration, I'm going to make the following assumptions:

1. You will work 48 weeks in the coming year at the very most. Each workday will be eight hours in length, and you will work five days a week. These figures total 1920 hours a year. For the simplicity of arithmetic, we'll round that up to a very reasonable number of 2000 hours.
2. A 'client' can be either a single person or a group of people such as a family.
3. Following this definition, your practice services 200 clients.
4. Your practice consists of a single advisor and one support staff member.

As you will see in Figure 1 on the next page, it takes roughly 800 hours each year – or 40% of your time – to manage the experience side of a 200-client practice. The rest of your time – 1200 hours – is spent with administration, continuing education, administration of existing business, compliance, branch meetings, and of course business development. As you can see, your 2000 hours will be accounted for very quickly.

You need to know how much of this available time – these 800 hours – you have to invest with *each* client. Knowing that all clients are not created equal is part of sculpting your division of labor.

In Figures 2 and 3 that follow, you can see two simple charts that segment clients by how much revenue they bring into your practice. Figure 2 are the rough numbers for a $200K grossing producer, and just because it seemed like fun, I've provided in Figure 3 the rough numbers for a $500K producer.

These charts also outline the suggested number of hours you spend with each client in each group, based on what percentage of revenue they bring to your practice.

Figure 1: Division of 2000-hour year

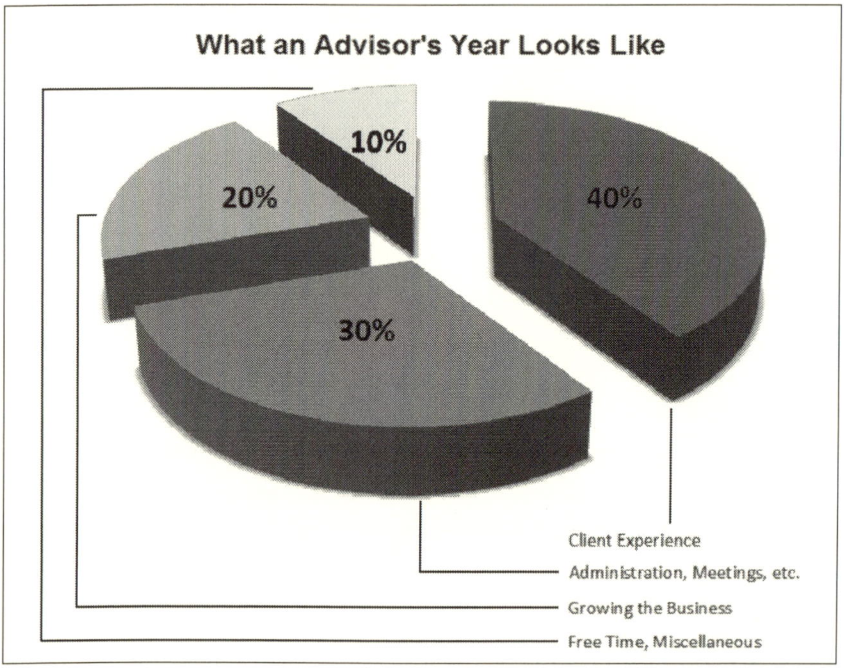

Looking at these tables, your 40 Platinum clients generate 50% of the revenue for the practice, and I believe that it is in your best interest to make sure you invest 50% of your time with them. We agree that it takes 800 hours to manage your clients, so if we follow the math, a Top 40 client should share 50% of your available time (400 hours) which is equal to 10 hours of service per client over a year (400 hours/40 clients). Not only should a Top 40 client receive 10 hours of your time, they should receive a proportional amount of your client management budget, which in this case is 1.25%.

Similarly and based strictly on revenue, you would spend 3.5 hours with the clients who generate 35% of your revenue (800 hours x 35%/80 clients) and 1.5 hours with those clients who generate 15% of your revenue (800 hours x 15%/80 clients).

Obviously, this segmentation is based purely on revenue and doesn't take into account attitude or the potential for referrals or for future revenue. Exceptions will be made because exceptions always are, and we

Figure 2: $200K/annum producer

# Of CLIENTS	TOTAL REVENUE	AVERAGE PER CLIENT REVENUE
PLATINUM - Top 40	50%	$2,500/year
GOLD - Mid 80	35%	$875/year
SILVER - Low 80	15%	$375/year

Figure 3: $500K/annum producer

# Of CLIENTS	TOTAL REVENUE	AVERAGE PER CLIENT REVENUE
PLATINUM - Top 40	50%	$6,250/year
GOLD - Mid 80	35%	$2,200/year
SILVER - Low 80	15%	$937/year

will get into what constitutes an ideal client profile, or top tier client, in a moment. For now, however, we are moving the big pieces into place so that you get an idea of what the big brush strokes look like.

So you have now solved one of the two major problems. You know how much time you will be spending with your 200 clients. And if you have fewer than 200 clients, I am of the belief that it is best for you to stay that way. The fewer clients you work with, the better your ability to provide an exceptional service, which we'll talk about in later chapters when we start putting your plan together.

Pretty simple, isn't it? You can make a chart for yourself similar to these samples, plugging in your numbers. I encourage you to do so. It is staggering when you start plotting out the lifetime value of clients over five and ten years. What is even more staggering is how this number becomes even higher when you factor in the value of a referral to a new client, and then that new client's value over ten years.

TIME SHIFT: THE ENTREPRENEURIAL TIME SYSTEM®[4]

I learned about Dan Sullivan's Entrepreneurial Time System® many years ago, and I have relied on it, benefited from it, referenced and recommended it ever since. I am a fan. I'm convinced that implementing this system into your life is essential.

Most people have jobs. Relatively few of us are self-employed.

People who have jobs live an entirely different existence from those who run businesses. They live in a nine-to-five time management system which requires uniformity, repetition, and predictability of activity and communication day after day and year after year. Everybody has to start work at the same time so that they can work with each other to get things done. Like the little dwarves in Disney's *Snow White*, we chisel away at our tasks, take our breaks and wish each other well at the end of the day. You can't have the printing department closed when the editing department is operating.

Most people will tell you that their workday is sometimes very busy and sometimes rather quiet. There are times when they make colleagues wait, and there are times when they are the ones left waiting. All kinds of time is wasted.

In contrast, entrepreneurs thrive on productivity, variety and creativity. Our job is not a "job." It's a lifestyle, and there are many hats to wear. Without a system in place, we are surely damned to failure. We simply will not be able to find the time to get it all done.

---

[4] Dan Sullivan, http://www.strategiccoach.com. The Entrepreneurial Time System® is a creation of The Strategic Coach founders, Dan Sullivan and Babs Smith. All references to the elements and workings of The Entrepreneurial Time System®, such as Focus Days, Buffer Days, Free Days, belong to The Strategic Coach, and its principles are used here with respect to the originators.

It's important, then, that you are focused on the key activities that are dedicated to achieving your goals. One of your goals might be growth, or it might be organization. It might be more personal freedom, and possibly, it might be all of the above. For your goals to be realized, you need to ensure you are doing the right things as often as possible, and learning a new way to manage time is an important shift.

How often have you allowed an interruption to take precedence over a task you are engaged in? Maybe the interruption is an inquiry, a phone call or an email. You efficiently deal with each interruption. But how long does it take you to refocus on what you were doing beforehand? A minute? Longer if you need to re-read, to get your thoughts back to where they once belonged? All those minutes add up.

From now on, you should break your week into specific classes of days, and do very specific tasks on those days so that you may focus on them completely. Consider these categories:

1. Focus Days
2. Buffer Days
3. Free Days

Focus Days are the days that you spend 80% of your time focusing on the activities, relationships and issues that matter most to your enterprise.

How do you determine what activities, relationships and issues matter most to your enterprise? Think about those categories in terms of which make the greatest contributions to your company's bottom line. Not surprisingly, you'll probably find that these are the activities that also energize you personally, which give you a sense of progress and accomplishment when you are engaged in them. Imagine how productive you could be if you were able to spend a day attending to just these tasks, without interruption, and with full preparation and support. This is what Focus Days are for, and Focus Days will represent your biggest block of time.

On Buffer Days, you handle all of the details that would otherwise distract your attention on a Focus Day. You use these days to catch up, clean up messes, send agendas, delegate duties and tasks. Buffer Days are also used for the personal matters in your life that are important, such as getting to the dry cleaner, renewing your company credit card, having your car serviced and paying your taxes.

Free Days are what you would assume. They are days completely free of work without exception. They are dedicated so that you may rejuvenate. Free Days are essential for managing energy, perspective and focus.

Yet while Free Days are critically important, most entrepreneurs don't take enough of them. When you fail to take time off to recharge, you become a liability to your business. When you refuse to take time, you are refusing to delegate tasks. Here are some of the results: progress stalls, your team stagnates, people stop learning, and you stop empowering.

When you run out of energy, you run out of creativity. Without creativity, you can't see nor seize opportunity. You risk harming the very creation you are trying to protect.

You should need – not want – your Free Days, and they should be planned and sacred.

Here's a little snapshot of a planned Free Day I was able to enjoy in the spring of 2012 in Banff National Park, Alberta. I was standing at the top of a mogul run on the slopes of the Lake Louise Mountain Resort, surrounded by my friends. We are all having the time of our lives: the day was perfect, the run was perfect, the snow was deep. It is so alive in my memory that I need to use the present tense. Everyone is laughing, everyone is shouting, there is an awful lot of creative (and sometimes salty) language being used. We howl like wolves. It is the most spectacular time I have ever spent skiing.

Days like this don't just happen. I plan them, I work for them and I scatter them around just frequently enough that I never have to wait for them too long before another comes along.

For the record, I spend at least 150 days a year travelling. Another 115 days of each year are spent in the office. Of these 115 office days, eighty are Focus Days, and the remainder are Buffer Days. I take one hundred days as free, sprinkling them throughout the year for recharging. A little later on, I will reference back to these days when we examine how you put your plan and processes together.

DO WHAT YOU DO BEST, DELEGATE THE REST

Based on revenue, the three smartest things that I can do in my business are speak, communicate on the telephone and write, whether the latter is leveraging social media in the form of blogs, tweets and Facebook updates, or working on a book. What about you? What are the three things that make the most sense for you to be doing all the time?

Conversely, what are the things you do that, when you find yourself doing them, make you want to pull your hair out? For me, it's dealing with details: setting up conference calls, booking flights or coordinating with event planners. At one time, I was so busy doing these tasks that I needed an entire day just to sort them away. I now delegate all of this to a process and a person whose talents lay in that area, and I keep them off my plate so that I can invest my energy where it does the most good and the least harm.

Wasting time can kill your enterprise, so it is essential that you only do what you should be doing and be as focused as possible. If you cannot afford an assistant, schedule a Buffer Day (or morning, if that is all that is needed) to deal with all inbound emails, meeting arrangements and other assorted important but non-essential activities. Otherwise, hire an assistant as soon as possible. The sooner you free yourself up to do what is most important to your enterprise, the better.

YOUR WEEK AT A GLANCE

You might wish to try the following suggestion: don't meet with anyone on Mondays. Use it instead as a Buffer Day in which you can prepare for your Focus Days, which are Tuesdays through Thursdays. Reserve each Friday so that it is available as either an additional weekly Buffer Day or as your Free Day whenever you feel the need to take one.

I once had a chat with an advisor who ran a successful practice. By his own admission, he told me that he was too busy and that he was burning out. So we talked a bit about the entrepreneurial workweek, and I laid out the exact week for him that I just described to you. Several months later, we met up at a conference, and he was a changed man. He had actually physically transformed. Gone was a lot of extra weight he'd been carrying, and the difference was striking. He told me that he attributed his renewal to the entrepreneurial workweek. He had not needed to give up a single client, he hadn't needed to hire more staff, and he hadn't committed to a better process.

All he had done was switch to the new work schedule we'd discussed. He told me that he went from being too busy, to actually having extra time. With that time, he started to ride his bike to work, something he really enjoyed, and this in turn inspired him to make a few changes to his diet. One thing accelerated into another, and by the time we were discussing this, he had lost thirty pounds. All of this from changing how he worked. He told me that, on the work front, everything had become easier and measurably better as a direct result.

I believe him because I've been there myself.

Remember what the bigger picture is – your desire to be a VSA who runs a world-class wealth management practice. Consider how effective you would be if you came in and did nothing but meet with clients all day long. Each meeting would have been planned, agendas sent, the client greeted, the room prepped, the script known. Similar to a dentist making her rounds, you simply move from appointment to appointment completely prepared and in control. Think about how much better your results would be, how much more efficient your day would be. Your management of time is going to be a big part of your success.

THE IDEAL CLIENT PROFILE

> "I don't want to change the world; I'm not looking for a new England, I'm just looking for another girl."
>
> — *Billy Bragg*

Let me put the ideal client concept into perspective for you.

There are millions of potential clients out there. You need two hundred or less of them to achieve your inspiring vision of success. Two hundred or less. One client with two million dollars is worth eight clients with $250,000. Simply put, it's not that hard.

Let's agree that there is no shortage of clients with whom you could work. The challenge, then, is in getting their attention and getting them to take action. Thankfully, it has never been easier for people to meet up and share with like-minded people. And you don't need a dating service to do it.

VSAs know this fact, so they focus their efforts on creating the very best experience for a very particular type of client. They don't chase numbers, they don't compromise, and they don't sell out. They focus all of their energy on servicing this client, on improving the client's experience and in creating opportunities for word to spread.

Out there, wandering around with their portfolios tucked under their arms, are two hundred people who could be the most fantastic clients you could ever wish for. They are waiting for you to get your act together. They are living with the status quo, wishing for something better. They would love your style, your clarity, your process and your attention. They would sleep better at night because you walk the earth and manage their money.

For the benefit of having a relationship with you, they would be willing to meet your conditions. They would attend your meetings and look forward to them. They would return your calls, defer to your expertise and empower you as their primary financial advisor. Your relationship with them would be built on mutual understanding and trust.

Sounds pretty good, doesn't it? Let's make it happen.

So far, you've prepared your strategy (your reason for being), your purpose and defined the business you are really in. If all has gone as anticipated, you have determined that the business you are really in is in clearing away people's financial concerns, the ones that cloud their thoughts and take up their energy. Through your careful financial planning, you have empowered your clients to stop worrying and start living.

Oh, I can hear you now. "Potential clients would consider me an idiot if I were to presume that I can help them learn how to live. What the heck does that even mean?"

Fair enough. For every cup, there's a saucer. But this is what I know: when I wrote the value proposition above, it resonated with me because it is *exactly* what I want from my advisor. I want to focus all my energy at being profitable when I am working so that I can take time off and be truly unplugged and engaged with my family when I am not. I want someone to give me a plan, update me on it, keep me informed about what's going on, and tell me what to do about it. I want to accept their word as gospel and quickly get back to doing what I know I need to be doing, which isn't worrying about my financial planning.

You only need your promise to resonate with two hundred people, and this is why it is so important that your promise resonate within you. You need to find what you do that is meaningful so that you can bring some intent into the experience.

Remember, all you need are two hundred like-minded people. To be a $500K producer, assuming you earn 1% on roughly $50M, you need two hundred people with an average portfolio size of $250K. You can work out the numbers any way you like, but you should start to see this a little differently.

SO HOW DO WE FIND THESE PEOPLE?

Ask yourself some questions. What characteristics of a potential client (or an existing one) do you find counterproductive to a sound working relationship? We call these *red flags*. They are the traits that will stall your business from moving forward. List them.

Then ask yourself the following questions so that you can identify what we like to term *alignment characteristics*. These are the traits that would promote trusting long-term client relationships:

1. How would you like to be treated?

2. How would you like your staff to be treated?
3. What is the client's overall attitude like?
4. Are you fully empowered as a client's exclusive trusted advisor?
5. Does the client respect you?
6. Do they show respect by returning phone calls promptly, by not cancelling meetings, etc.?
7. Do they take your advice?

Consider now the assets you need to manage. How much does a client need to have, in terms of revenue or assets, in order to work with you? The minimum requirement for either is important because you need to earn a base level of compensation to make the relationship worthwhile. There is no right or wrong answer here. Whether you work in terms of revenue or assets, just be sure you are consistent. Quantify them in terms of *x* dollars within *y* period of time.

Next, consider the potential for a client to generate one or more referrals. Consider, too, the value of a client who currently has few assets but who stands to either inherit or generate a considerable amount.

CLIENT SEGMENTATION: PART DEUX

Whether you are looking to segment your existing client base or are in the process of building one, you should develop several categories, or tiers, of clients based on specific criteria. Earlier we had segmented clients into the categories of Platinum, Gold and Silver. In the figure that follows, I've further divided Platinum clients to show the variations that can exist within this segment.

Figure 4: Client Platinum Tier Subdivisions

Level	Tier	Client Attributes
Platinum	Tier 1	• Refer regularly (at least once a year for the past number of years) • In the top 50% of revenue • Meet your alignment criteria
Platinum	Tier 2	• In the top 50% of revenue • Meet alignment criteria
Platinum	Tier 3	• In the top 50% of revenue • Not fully aligned • May have one or more red flags • They are your client because of the income you generate from them
Gold	Tier 4	• 35% of revenue • Meet your alignment criteria • May or may not refer • Tier 2 without the assets/revenue
Silver	Tier 5	• The bottom 15% of revenue • Anyone from Tier 3 or 4 who is not a fit for your business

DENNIS MOSELEY-WILLIAMS AS AN IDEAL CLIENT CASE STUDY

Given your strategy, your reason for being, why would I make a good client for you? Who am I, beyond someone who owns $250K, and why do you think I would be interested in your promise?

I own a business. I have more sophisticated financial planning needs than a lot of people. I have banking, investing, business banking, insurance, personal accounting, business accounting and so much government reporting in Canada and the United States that it requires a full-time person and three related professionals.

I'm a small business owner, so I absolutely need an advisor who understands what I deal with every day. I need an advisor who can explain to me how they are going to take it all into consideration and present me with a solution. The fact that they can manage all of this for a small fee is completely appealing.

I am married with two daughters and a dog. My wife is a stay-at-home mom; before the children came along, she was a teacher. You can assume – correctly – that having a parent at home is important to us. I will also require educational savings plans for my girls.

We have a cabin in the woods, and I engineer my year to allow me to spend significant time there alone and with my family. Legacy and family are important to me; the cabin is a place where I have a lot of memories and do a lot of thinking.

That is pretty much what you would already have or should have captured about who I am in my CLAN (**C**areer/**L**ifestyle/**A**ctivities/**N**ext-of-kin) profile which lives in your contact manager. That is absolutely what a VSA would have written in my file, no question. Not only that, they would have made sure that every team member is able to access it and add or edit information. We'll get into data capture further on in the book.

The question now is: do you want to work with a client like me? If you are really inspired to help people take control of their worry and channel their energy toward a more fulfilling life, then I would say that I fit that profile.

So right there, I am aligned with your promise.

Let's assume that your ideal client profile is based on someone like me. You would therefore identify the following:

> *Your clients will be successful professionals and/or entrepreneurs who are in their thirties and forties and who are looking for a financial advisor to serve as their Personal CFO. You would manage all of their investments and serve as a financial counsel. Your clients have investable assets of $250K or more, are married and have legacy issues.*
>
> *Your ideal clients value your process, clarity and exceptional experience because they find it easy, clear, pleasant and enjoyable.*

Your ideal clients take their careers seriously. They want to protect and grow their assets and plan for the future. They value family time, education and legacy.

You've now identified your ideal clients.

When you create a single process that is appealing to your ideal clients, repeating the process becomes very simple and predictable. This process serves to back up your promise, which we determined in this case was to clear away financial concerns, educate, and empower so that your clients could enjoy the journey a little more and play a little more often.

RECAP

The resource management of your practice can become handicapped if you fail to identify and allow sufficient time to execute core deliverables. Adopting an entrepreneurial workweek that segments time more efficiently is an effective and recommended strategy for recovering the time needed.

Client segmentation based upon a specific set of variables further hones administration and management resources by letting you know which clients should receive specific time and services within the boundaries of the Client Experience.

Identifying the attributes of the Ideal Client to develop a common profiling description streamlines your practice so that your menu of resources and deliverables is not spread over a wide cross section of individuals with dissimilar needs.

Chapter 5

Formulating Your Experience Matrix

IF YOU HAVEN'T ALREADY, you are close to realizing that, as far as your practice is concerned, you may need to undertake a broad transformation, or 'sea change', a descriptive little term that Shakespeare left us. Brace yourself. Your Lizard may be more than a little on edge right now because a serious threat is afoot. He may be throwing up objections about how you never get past this point, the one where you realize you can't change, where you start to question how you are actually going to pull this off.

You will succeed for a few key reasons and that is all. Actually, that is everything.

1. You have a willingness to do the work. You *finish*. You do what you say you are going to do, you finish your work and you ship, which is just another way of saying you deliver on it.
2. You are motivated to be the very best version of yourself. You understand that time is short and that you've got one chance to get it right.
3. You run a good business. You know what that business is, you have

an existing plan in place, and you might even understand some Jedi sorcery as far as strategy, experience and alignment are concerned.

4. You are accountable. You can answer specific questions about your business easily. You focus 80% of your time doing what you should do. You organize your time differently, and every single client experience is driven by process and measured for success and adjustment.

This is the foundation. From here on forward, I will assume that you now have these fundamentals in place or ready to put into place so that your implementation may result in why you are in business in the first place: for an increased return on investment.

It is time to get your new plan started.

You have three groups of clients who have been segmented based on revenue per client. So those who pay you 50% are getting 10 service hours/year, those who generate 35% receive 3.5 service hours/year, and those clients who only generate 15% will receive 1.5 service hours/year. As you move through this chapter, it might be a good idea to keep a pad of paper handy so that you may fill out the activities you want to put into your plan based on segmentation.

You have two hundred clients or thereabouts, and some of them are more than one person, a couple for instance. Each one of these client units is very important because you care about all of your people. The reason you care about all of your people is because you have decided that the business you are really in:

Clears away people's financial concerns that cloud their thoughts and take up their energy, empowering them, through your financial planning, to stop worrying and start living.

COMMIT TO THE ESSENTIALS FIRST, WORRY ABOUT THE DETAILS LATER

The Lizard uses the details and a desire for perfection as reasons to stall. When you arrive upon an idea that makes sense, just start. Started, imperfect-but-in-the-air is more impressive and inspiring than anything languishing on the drawing board.

Your plan has to ensure that your clients empower you with all of their money, that they trust your process, and they send you referrals. For this to happen, you have to appeal to both their left and right brain sensibilities. You need to have a detailed process in place that lays out what is expected of you, which is financial planning, and furthermore, you need a process in place to help you monitor and nurture existing relationships that enhance the likelihood for referrals. Absolutely everything you do in your business will only be done if it helps you keep your promise.

Remember what your clients want from you:

1. An advisor who explains complicated concepts easily.
2. An advisor who checks in regularly.
3. An advisor who manages their expectations.

Your plan then must deliver an exceptional financial planning experience, while also allowing you to build and expand relationships with your existing clients and desired new clients.

So let's start with the core services you are going to provide your clients: financial information.

Review Meetings and Financial Planning

Will regularly scheduled meetings with your top clients help them feel more at ease and more free of stress and worry? Yes! They absolutely will! So you must regularly schedule review meetings with your clients, and the number of meetings they receive in any given year is determined by where they place in your client segmentation. Since every client gets a review meeting, it only stands to reason that your top clients might get two or three. How and where you conduct those additional meetings will be determined by the particular experience you wish to provide.

Reporting

When will your statements be delivered, and will they be paper or electronic? How frequently will they be sent out, and will they be sent according to a predictable, set schedule? Are your clients going to have online access to this information 24/7? Under what circumstances or conditions would the arrival of the statement (or imminent arrival) warrant a heads-up telephone call from your office? Will you send additional updates outside of your regular schedule when dramatic financial circumstances warrant it, such as a severe market correction or a catastrophic event, just to ease peace of mind?

Financial/Economic Client Events

Should you bring in an economist to speak to your clients? Let's think about this one. Your clients already get their economic updates from you; they already interpret the financial world through your filter. Do you want to confuse the message? Hiring the economist to speak to your clients may be a mistake. It may not be aligned with your message, so perhaps foregoing the economist and bringing in an estate settlement lawyer might serve your clients' needs more specifically. Therefore, consider *tailoring* client events of financial interest (because you will be hosting client events of other interest) to augment your services: education planning, tax reduction, estate planning, executor roles and so forth.

Additional Financial Communication

Will you send articles of financial interest to your clients? Will they be generic in nature, meaning that all clients across your segmentation might find them interesting? Would they be specific in nature, meaning, for instance, that business owner clients might receive a financial article about a new corporate tax law coming being passed? This is where a finely-tuned database that captures client-specific information about their interests and activities can serve you well.

There is a lot to consider; don't let it overwhelm you. You will master this in stages, laying down layer after layer of increasing detail and consideration. The Lizard wants you to stop, to think it's complicated when it's not, especially when you are considerate and measured in your thoughts and approach.

You may have just discovered that your bottom eighty clients – the ones who receive 1.5 hours of your time per year – have each now consumed all of that time with the some of the items mentioned in the categories above: an annual meeting, monthly reports, one or two financially-specific mailers about an investment vehicle they own, and your time on a few phone calls they make to you. That's okay. You are meeting all the benchmarks of your relationship while continuing to bring them value, and you are gaining current information for and during your annual reviews.

You may also find that among this bottom group are clients who are so removed from your Ideal Client Profile that it might serve your interests (and theirs) to divest so that you can dedicate your energy and resources to those who are better suited. We'll get into client right-sizing a little later on, but for now, simply consider the idea that you may not be the advisor that every client needs.

You've now thought about your core financial service obligations to your clients. What about non-financial considerations that are just as essential when it comes to building a holistic client experience? What else are you going to mail your clients throughout the year, and at what frequency? Holiday greetings? Birthday cards and anniversary letters? What about recognizing investment milestones or career promotions? Will you acknowledge other important events and milestones in their lives? Are you going to invite clients to any events this year? Do you even host client events? Do you plan to track their interests and send out articles they may find illuminating that are of non-financial but very personal interest?

We are going to plan a great year for you, your clients and your prospective clients. It will be one that will deliver an experience that will appeal to both your clients' desire for a professional financial planning process that is clear, understood and valued, as well as their desire for a personalized, pleasant relationship with you. Over several years, your clients are going to pay you a tremendous amount of money for you to deliver on these promises. In return, you want them to be your clients for life, to empower you as their personal CFO, to trust in your counsel and process, and to refer you to others who are looking for the same experience you offer.

DELIVERING SERVICE IS ONE THING. DELIVERING EXPERIENCE IS SOMETHING ELSE ALTOGETHER.

Dan the Painter

I own a rental property whose interiors once needed repainting. Although it's a nice home, I knew that, with tenant wear-and-tear, this would be a job that would be repeated every few years, so I didn't want to break the bank. A young man named Dan was recommended to me.

You might know this already, but painting – like plumbing – is one of those things that *should* be really easy but gets complicated far too quickly. Painters arrive late; they can't start until next week; the job ends up being sloppy. In my years as a landlord, I have heard and seen it all.

So when I met Dan, a fresh-faced young man, I was concerned. His price seemed right, maybe a little too right. It was enough to make me wonder if I was being foolish. Maybe I was about to throw good money out the window to save a few hundred dollars.

Dan walked through the entire house, asking me questions, and then he promised to send a proposal the next day. Sure enough, the following day, he emailed me an overview of the entire project, which included a timeline for when it would be completed and a budget for my consideration. In it, he essentially addressed every question I could have had about the project. When will it start? When will it finish? What happens between the day I hire you and the day you return the keys? I need to show the unit, so can you keep it tidy?

Dan's proposal wasn't exactly rocket science; it was straightforward and simple. But because most painters don't take the extra time to put together a nice proposal, it stood out and solidified my choice. More importantly, it put my mind at ease.

While Dan was painting the house, I showed it to prospective tenants. Every time, I would apologize in advance and remind the potential tenant that the home was being painted for them. I pointed out that they may have to step over a can of paint or, heaven forbid, walk under a ladder.

Yet every single time I brought a prospective client into the house, Dan's tools were laid out neatly on a sheet like a surgeon's. All of his tools were wiped clean, the cans organized. There were no coffee cups, sandwich wrappers or garbage of any kind lying about. I could literally look at his timeline, see what he had done (because it was exactly what he had said he would do). I knew when he was gone for the day. This happened every night.

I truly think that Dan helped me rent that house. Because of his work, I looked like the kind of landlord who delivered on quality and took care of things. As much as I wanted to trust my tenants, they needed to know that they could trust me. Based on the painter I'd hired, I have to believe they were put at ease.

After the job was done, Dan sent my wife and me flowers and thanked us for hiring him. Frankly, Dan had me at the job quote, but the flowers anchored him as a person. He was no longer a painter; he was Dan the Painter, and we have used him again since.

Last year, I spent about $40K on cars, and that guy didn't send me flowers. I spent $30K on real estate fees, and that guy didn't send me flowers. I spent about $12K on groceries and not only did they not give me flowers, they sold me flowers. I spent $2K painting a house, and the painter thought my trust was important enough to send me flowers.

I believe there is a lesson in this little story for all of us.

When you opt to work with a client such as myself, then it is understood that you will fulfill all of my financial planning needs. A personal CFO is *expected* to do this. I don't think of how lucky I am that you do succession planning – I expect you to do succession planning. I wouldn't have hired you otherwise.

I'm not going to be surprised if you know an accountant who specializes in Canadians who do business in the USA, or immigration lawyers who work with consultants who have the work visa I have. Why would I be surprised? You are a good financial advisor who specializes in working with people like me. I would expect you to know these other professionals.

What isn't expected or assumed (and is therefore appreciated) is your attention to the other details that are big emotional issues for me. Things like how often you check in with me and the sense you give me that you care and are in control. Finally, and in no way less important, I endlessly appreciate how well you manage the experience. You'll never hear me singing *You Don't Bring Me Flowers Anymore.*

Your attention to these details is the magic of the experience that you are delivering. Every advisor in the world is going to get a client the returns required or else the advisor will be replaced. Achieving the financial goal of the plan is expected and essential.

How it feels to be your client, how it feels to be taken care of by you, the ratio of stressful moments to peaceful moments, however, is what your client will ultimately measure when they consider endorsing you.

The Hair Salon

I have a pretty simple haircut. I am losing my hair so I keep cutting it shorter and shorter. That way, no one will really be surprised when it finally disappears. It's best described as 'neat', as in tidy and not hip. Hip and I parted ways years ago after an argument because I said, "I'd rather be comfortable." A cut costs me about $15, which is frankly a lot of money given the non-technical nature of the work involved. It's a clipper job.

On a day in which I was scrambling to get out of town on business, I couldn't get to my own barber. I had no option but to go to my wife's salon, which was nearby.

When I raced in, I was told that, without an appointment, they weren't able to help me. They were polite but it was unequivocally a no. I didn't know what to do and just stood there, my little bit of hair still slowly growing. I was saved by the owner, Frank, who recognized me as the husband of one of his very good clients. Frank said he'd look after me shortly.

Suddenly, everything changed.

I didn't have to think about what to do, where to go or what came next because I was now taken into their care. Within an instant, my mind shifted from urgency and time constraints to being completely relaxed. My jacket was lifted from my shoulders, and I was offered a choice of coffee or latte, which I accepted. I sat down and chuckled a little at being the only fox among the hens as it were, but then the naturally curious professional in me took over.

I have to admit, I felt like an anthropologist, doing my best to blend in, to appear "local", flipping through a magazine without a care in the world while carefully observing this curious rite of passage.

I tried to envision what it would be like if this were the first time I was seeing the business. I noted where people were, what they were doing, what they were saying, the art on the walls, the music coming from the speakers, which was cool, as was the entire vibe of the place. It was an oasis. It could have been a night club off a hotel lobby except for the bright sunlight outside. It was about escaping to an experience that was all about feeling beautiful and good. People were happy, and why shouldn't they be? Every client had a team of professionals crawling all over them.

This is nothing like a barber shop, where the promise is to cut your hair and get you in and out. For the first time, I realized that the purpose of a salon is to *stay*. The purpose is to take your time, to feel like you are somewhere special. Not for the first time, it occurred to me that women are pretty awesome.

Eventually it was my turn, and I was lead away. They washed my hair, talked to me, put a hot cloth on my face, massaged my scalp, all the while asking me questions about my wife, what I did for a living, sharing with me what they were up to. All in all, we spent about ten minutes together having a nice little human connection.

Then it was my turn with Frank. It was like a procession after the show I had just had at the sinks. I was more than a little curious to know how he was going to cut what hair I had. Frank sat me down, covered me with a heavier apron than I wear at the barber's. So far so good. This was different! Then, clippers in hand, he cut my hair in five minutes, just like my barber does.

All the pretty things aside, it came down to the same clippers, same moves, same time invested, same cut. The only difference was that the haircut cost me $50 instead of $15, and he wasn't complaining in my ear in a heavy accent about city taxes.

Next thing I knew, the cut was over, I had paid, tipped and been handed my coat with the offer of a coffee to go, which I accepted. Standing outside on a busy downtown street, the wind blowing in my face, I did not think, surprisingly, "You've just been had!" Rather, I found myself wondering as I sipped my coffee, why I would deny myself that little pleasure every once in a while. So what if I paid too much for a wash I didn't need, a coffee and to hear that my kids were cute.

Your obligation is to fulfill your promise. So whenever it makes sense, when the innovation improves the experience for your client, then I suggest that you are obligated to make that change and to incorporate it into your process. This is what innovation is: a commitment to improvement.

I will assume that you have committed yourself to working on what you do best as opposed to spending energy chasing prospects. This is what separates the VSA – and I daresay you very soon – from everyone else. You know the business you are in, you know your clients, you know how much time to spend with each of them, you know what they value, and you spend as much of your time as possible making all of it better.

YOUR PLAN IS ABOUT THEIR MONEY AND MOODS

We know that you now have three segmented groups of clients who are rated from most important to least important as determined by revenue. You have to spend either 10, 3.5 or 1.5 hours annually with each of them to exceed their expectations of you as a professional.

Your plan has to accomplish two goals. The first is to establish with new clients or reinforce with existing clients your credibility as a financial professional. Your financial planning process has to be clear, and the uniqueness of your personal approach has to be understood. It is critical to your long-term success that you manage your clients' expectations by ensuring you address any unspoken questions or concerns.

People don't always like to share that they are confused or do not understand. To save face, they might act like they understand everything you tell them, but in point of fact they have unanswered questions and some lingering uneasiness. These sorts of feelings are toxic; they can grow and corrupt the relationship.

Your plan also has to accommodate a communication schedule that strengthens your existing relationships and creates a sense of belonging and comfort for your clients. Remember, you have to know what their money is for.

This is why you need a call rotation. You might have noticed that a call rotation wasn't in the list of core services earlier in this chapter, but that's not because it doesn't belong there. I was saving it for this section because it perfectly illustrates how your voice, your phone call, is an excellent example how you are able to link the emotional and logical aspects of how your clients perceive you. In this texting and tweeting world, nobody seems to understand the value of a telephone call. You have one thing that every other advisor in town would like to have, and that is permission to call your client. You want to use this opportunity as appropriately and perfectly as possible.

Your call rotation is a quarterly event in which you touch base to find out what's new. Not only that, the call rotation keeps you current with your clients' money in motion. In preparation for the call, review previous calls and the information in your CLAN history so that you are able to pull details to build upon. Then use a script. For example, you may want to ask whatever came of that 1950s Oldsmobile the client was looking at buying from his uncle so he could restore it. Did he and his wife end up taking the Greek island cruise? Did they ever sort out the kitchen cupboard issue in their cottage renovations?

There are two objectives here. Build relationships, and become aware of any money in motion: new events, expenses, promotions, inheritances. This is where you really learn what their money is for, what their future hopes and plans are.

Blocking time so that these calls can be grouped allows you to be in the right physical space and the right mental place so that you can then do smart things. If a client tells you that they are really excited because they will be running in an upcoming half-marathon, buy them a book on running. If someone tells you that they are fulfilling a life-long dream and taking a vacation to the Galapagos, send them web links of interest. Share their excitement. Show them you care.

Record all information, and make sure that the members of your team reference these facts in future conversations.

Whenever you are speaking with a client and financial matters come up, use a tactic that the best educators have long known and employed. Don't wait for your client to ask about something they don't understand, and don't assume that they even know what the questions are. Ask your client questions that require them to tell you about a particular investment strategy or investment function that is pertinent to their portfolio. If they can describe it, then you know they understand it. If they cannot, then you have uncovered another teaching opportunity. Consider these inquiries little educational tune-ups. They serve to open dialogue, and they position you as being vigilant about your clients' financial acumen and well-being. They tell the client that your relationship is a partnership and that they are an active player.

In Chapter Four, when we examined the Ideal Client Profile, we proposed an Ideal Client as:

> *Successful professionals and/or entrepreneurs in their thirties and forties and who are looking for a financial advisor to serve as their Personal CFO. You manage all of their investments and serve as a financial counsel. Your clients have investable assets of $250K or more, are married and have legacy issues.*
>
> *More than anything, they want peace in their financial world so that they can focus on what is most important to them: their business and family. They always worry that they spend too much time working, so they are looking for some confidence that they can afford to*

take this time off, unplug and enjoy life. They value reporting, updates and education.

Once again I will remind you that the above is only an example. You can work with whomever you desire, and you should find this work meaningful and enjoyable.

Let's go back and revisit how I might be in your Ideal Client Profile. I am an entrepreneur, self-employed, and I can cover your $250K requirement, so this is good. However, what you will find is that the answer to, "How do I keep DMW happy and talking about me?" isn't driven by the financial side of our relationship because as we have agreed or should agree, when I hire you I expect you to fulfill your obligation.

The food is always good, the waiter is the reason you recommend.

As your Ideal Client, the money I have invested with you is for my future retirement. My mad money is for ski trips and days at my cabin. Everything about what I do is ultimately to spend time on a ski hill or at the lake with my friends and family.

Your secret is that you follow a process to make sure the left brain issues are solved: planning, reporting, measuring, and adjusting. Not only that, you see your obligation as having to make the client experience as perfect and as customized as possible. You understand this, and you know that managing the assets is much easier and less time-consuming than managing the person.

So when you are thinking about your plan and putting together the lists of activities with which you want to fill your ten hours, you might want to consider articles of interest that you can easily get from your client's profile.

On a quarterly basis, you might send your top clients an article that relates to a personal interest. My advisor has sent me a lot of information on cottages and cabins since I purchased one six years ago. Some of them are fun items: recipes, things to do with kids, family-oriented bits of trivia, like how to keep your beach safe. I got a lot of value out of one article he sent on insurance. But what I really get from these mailings is a reminder that I am understood, that what makes me unique is taken into consideration, and that I am not receiving a generic approach to planning or experience.

A while back, I met an advisor who had been working on securing a prospect for a number of years. They had met socially a few times and had discussed the merits of an appointment. But the meeting was never really important enough for the prospect to commit.

This story was typical, and I have certainly heard a version of it hundreds of times: how does one get a prospect, who has been met socially, to sit down and consider becoming a client?

As the story goes, the advisor knew that the prospect was a father who owned either a ski property or a time share near Vail. One day, the advisor was having a coffee at his desk and reading through his new copy of *SKI* magazine, whose cover story was titled, "How to Raise a Skier." As the advisor later related to me, "Without thinking, I just stood up and photocopied the cover and the article. I stuffed both in an envelope with a note that read, *You are probably thinking about this right now,* and I mailed it to the prospect."

The advisor stressed to me that he would never normally do this sort of thing, mail a prospect such a non-financial article with a note. He said he listens to guys like me and loves the message, but he never ever implements. He admitted that he also doesn't ever send birthday cards, anniversary cards or anything of the sort, which was why he was so adamant that I understand how out of the norm it was that he would spontaneously send this article.

Within two weeks, the prospect called, apologizing for not having replied sooner and asking for an appointment. The prospect said that the article had really meant a lot to him. He said that his youngest daughter was just getting onto skis for the first time, that his other children were older and that he was fully aware of how this might be the last time he would be skiing with one of his kids. He added that he felt it might be his last kick at the parenting can and that he and his wife were suffering from a little empty nest syndrome.

What made the article so powerful, and which may have been why the advisor felt compelled to send it along, was that the article made the point that to raise a skier, you first have to understand the goal. The goal isn't to teach a child how to ski; it is to teach them that you, the parent, are fun to hang out with. Because any ski instructor can teach your children to ski. But only you, the parent, can make sure that *you* are fun and patient, that when they want to quit, you quit and not beg them to do another run. It's the parent who can laugh a lot, who – when everyone on the slopes wants to stop to eat exactly at noon, at the exact busiest time of the day – says, "Good idea!" and then offers to stand in line while they go inside to warm up even though it's not cold.

So the article nailed the prospect right in the part of his brain and heart that said, "Holy smokes, life goes fast, and I'm down to one little girl left at home, and where did my other kids get to?" The shift he made after receiving the article was that he felt, "This advisor *understands* me."

I literally get chills writing that.

At the risk of being completely convenient, this advisor went on to follow a New Client Welcome Process he had once heard our company recommend. He landed the client, which included the client's entire portfolio. Within a few months, the advisor provided this new client's mother with an estate plan. Since 2010, when I met this advisor, he has received two additional referrals from the elusive prospect, and in each case the new prospects have mentioned "the magazine story." We connect over stories. The new clients are making a judgment about the advisor based on his savvy to send that article. Before they even meet him, they have decided that he is a good and well-meaning person.

What this tells us is that when the new client talks about him, he doesn't talk about returns or process. He talks about the magazine article and how his advisor understands him.

Seth Godin wrote in his excellent blog that people believe nothing that you tell them but everything they tell themselves."[5]

The story about the magazine article is powerful because it is real. We can all envision it, we can all appreciate it. It means more to us than, "My advisor works with business owners and generated 9.6% in returns last year."

---

[5] Seth Godin, *Belief*, http://sethgodin.typepad.com/seths_blog/2006/07/belief.html (July 29, 2006).

Think back to Dan the Painter. Every person I have referred him to comments on how he arranges the tools at his worksite. When we talk about Dan, they don't say, "He is a good painter." What they say is, "He is meticulous and exact." They regard Dan as being more than the job he does. The good paint job he produces is a fact and an important one. But the way he does it makes something that is intangible become something that is real. And while we care about the quality of the fact, whether it's Dan the Painter or you the advisor, it's nowhere near as compelling as the experience of what you each deliver.

AFTER BUILDING THE FOUNDATION, FRAME IT UP

So the foundation is poured, the floor is laid, and now it's time to erect a simple frame so that by the end of the day you can walk around your new structure with some idea of where the rooms and hallways go. Suddenly what was just a hole in the ground is beginning to resemble something else – your vision.

What needs to happen now are the finishing touches, those details that mirror our taste and make us feel comfortable. This can be the slow and expensive stuff. It can also be the most frustrating. At this point, I anticipate a full-on attack by the Lizard, complete with whining and desires on your part for all kinds of sinful things, which may or may not begin with bad food. Speaking personally, I'm not kidding about that one. When I am working on something important, I want all kinds of food that isn't in my house as I near the breakthrough. The Lizard is trying to get me to take a break and go get what I want, hoping that the break in momentum will save him. It's the same thing as calling a time-out to 'ice the kicker' before a critical field goal. The Lizard will want to distract you once he suspects you have defeated self-doubt.

So let's get the framing done. If you have not yet filled out the basics for what you will do with your three tiers of segmented clients, do it now. We are about to take each of those essentials and break them down to see what they are, how they work, and how we can make them better. It's time for more innovation.

Your goals for each client are that they empower you as their primary financial advisor, trust in you and your process, and also refer when the opportunity arises.

This means that everything you plan to do needs to be done as well as possible. Other advisors host meetings with clients, but you host meeting events. Other advisors get through their call rotations as if they were chores, whereas you see them as incredible opportunities for gathering information on your clients, tracking money in motion and for reinforcing relationships.

This means that you are going to need a process that lays out what you want to do and specifies how you plan to do it so that it is consistently executed every single time. In the next chapter, we will look at how to build your process. For the time being, I just want you to think about how to make your essentials better.

Have someone ready to greet your clients when they arrive for meetings.

Frank, an advisor I met in New Jersey, told me that he always has someone waiting to meet his clients when they arrive for a meeting. "It's important for the client to know that we are expecting them, that they understand we consider their presence a big deal." His rationale is that, while he as an advisor might consider what he does for the client to be important, the fact of the matter is that clients don't tend to think of their advisors very often except when it comes to discussing business related to their account. They are too busy living their lives. Having someone greet them counters that notion. It says, "We think about you all the time because you are important to us. So important, in fact, that your arrival commands our attention."

Stage your meetings as if you worked on Broadway.

Your client meetings need to be staged just like a theatre production. Imagine that your client has arrived (on a Tuesday through Thursday because you adhere to an entrepreneurial workweek), and they have been greeted by name with a smile and a handshake. If there are coats, they've been taken and hung. If your client needs assistance of any kind, that has been offered and provided. They are escorted to where the meeting will take place.

Whether that meeting is in your office or in the boardroom is your choice. Once that is decided, you need to prepare. Desk surfaces are uncluttered and spare; this is not the time to use props to show how busy you are. An agenda has been printed and awaits you and your client. You have a meeting outline prepared for yourself as well to guide your speaking points and upon which to make notes. It is up to you whether you choose to plug data into your computer at the meeting. To some clients, computer input can be off-putting because it reduces eye contact, so use your judgment.

You have offered beverages which your assistant can provide once the client has decided on what they'd like or which are available nearby if you work without an assistant. Because you are attentive to these things, you have a plate of baked goods available that were bought that morning and which are refreshed before each meeting. If you are particularly attentive and record your CLAN information carefully, you will have offered the right food choices to someone who is diabetic, celiac or vegan. That observance of their unique needs speaks volumes about how much attention you pay to them.

If you meet in a boardroom, you may have laid a table cloth beneath the flatware, glassware and the real – not paper – dishes you have set out. Your selection of beverages and snack items are nearby. Fresh flowers will be in the room. You'll have additional linens in case there are spills. The napkins may be seasonal, of special paper or plain.

All of this is simply your scenery staging, but it is no less important just because it is in the background. It is another stitch in the experience you are knitting, building upon the personal greeting and the escort to your meeting place. Now you are ready to get down to the purpose of your event.

Do you disagree that your top clients are worth this extra effort? Remember that a top client receives ten hours of your time in a given year; they may pay you hundreds of dollars an hour if not thousands.

I attended a meeting in San Diego one time, in which the advisor asked me if I wanted to see his client onboarding process, something that he called 'Show Time'. At this point, we were already a few hours into our meeting, and once we wrapped up, he demonstrated to me how he meets a new client.

I was brought out to the lobby and asked to wait. About five minutes later, one of his assistants came and met me as if we had never met before. She had a big smile, nice handshake, lots of enthusiasm. "Mr. Moseley-Williams," she said. "I'm Karen, and I'm so happy you are here. We are all looking forward to meeting you."

Karen brought me to the advisor's suite of offices. As I approached, each member of the team stood and approached me, shook my hand, introduced themselves and told me what they did. "Hi Mr. Moseley-Williams, I am Kate Edwards, and I am one of the two people on the team who manages our custom portfolios. I'm really happy to meet you."

This continued until everyone was standing around me, smiling, and then the advisor approached. All the team members parted like the Red Sea, and the advisor said, "Hi, I'm Ajay, and we are all happy you are here. Let's go into my office."

Ajay brought me to his office where I was invited to sit at a corner table. As soon as I had taken my seat, Karen came into the room and placed to one side of the table a lovely large silver tray laden with every conceivable refreshment you can imagine. Ajay excused himself, telling me he would be back in two minutes. He invited me to help myself and be comfortable.

Exactly two minutes later, Ajay returned and asked me what I thought of his welcome experience. I asked him if he typically went anywhere during those two minutes, and he laughed. "Sometimes," he said. "Just as often, I stand there counting down on my watch. What's important is that I give the client time to become comfortable and reflect on what has happened, let them take it all in."

Ajay's welcome process remains one of the most impressive I have ever encountered.

Ajay knows what business he is really in. He is in the business of making people feel cared for and important, and everything he does drives home those points. He knows that his clients have as much as ten – or as little as one and a half – hours of his office's time and that every moment is an opportunity to reinforce his message and to fulfill his promise.

Which is better, which has more value – a meeting, or a meeting that is part of a process? A meeting, or a meeting that is enjoyable to attend, where work gets done but everybody is tuned in and focused?

Mix it up: Consider hosting some meetings offsite so that they become an event.

Give your clients an experience to look forward to and a memory to talk about.

In addition to having a staff member greet his clients, Frank also meets clients for reviews at an appropriate restaurant, one that is also the site of larger events he hosts. These are usually the second or third meeting with a client in a given year, not the primary financial review, and the venue matches the comfort level of Frank's relationship with the client. The owners of this restaurant therefore appreciate his business and graciously greet his clients when they arrive for a scheduled appointment. Frank may combine these review meetings with a larger function that he has scheduled for around the same time. For example, he may conduct three independent reviews mid-morning and then move directly into a larger invitation-only client luncheon whose purpose might be a matter of either financial interest or a topic recreational in nature. When the luncheon is over, Frank remains at the restaurant for additionally scheduled independent reviews.

I was actually so impressed with this idea that I have since incorporated it into my own business routine, particularly when I am travelling to a city whose geography I am unfamiliar with. Sometimes, when I fly in for a speaking presentation, advisors ask to meet with me on other matters prior to the event. It is important that the energy I need for my presentation not be sapped by negotiating with the local taxi drivers, travelling from one meeting site to another, waiting around. It is a far more relaxing and a productive use of time for advisors to come to me. If they are running a little late, I have my laptop fired up for other tasks I can be working on. So I'll situate in the hotel restaurant, acquaint myself with the wait staff, tip them generously so that they may take care of me (which can be expensed), and I'm ready to go. Then, as the day wears on until my scheduled presentation, I am able to sit in a nice restaurant and meet with my clients. After each meeting, the waitress can whisk over, tidy up, change the linens, and fifteen minutes later, my next appointment arrives. It's all very efficient, pleasant and affords the advisors a welcomed break from their routines.

Getting back to Frank, he told me that if he is only going to see his clients three times a year and that none of them will attend any client events, he needs to make sure that he can provide these clients with at least one experience that is, in his words, "more than good. I want it to be the event they won't otherwise have with me."

An appointment is something you do with your dentist, and you end it by spitting in a sink. An event is something you look forward to, learn from and talk about.

An event is when you walk in with the expectation that "this will be awesome" and walk out thinking about new possibilities. A meeting, by contrast, is something you have with your accountant who explains to you your tax bill, or with a municipal official who tells you why the otherwise healthy tree in your front yard needs to be cut down.

Schedule your meetings with clarity and predictability.

When you look over your calendar for the next twelve months, your meetings should be scheduled so that you know when you will be seeing every one of your clients. When a meeting is concluding, let the client know you'll be seeing them again in twelve months (or three or four, depending on the client tier) and that they'll receive a reminder beforehand. When they leave, you or your assistant enters the recurring activity into your CRM, which includes the pre-meeting scheduling call and the sending of the agenda. Never be ambivalent about the scheduling of your next meeting. Don't say, "I'll call you in the Fall and see about getting together." Nobody should ever wonder when they are going to see you. You do a lot of damage to your client relationships and your perceived value when you are casual about booking appointments.

Why the agenda? You do not want your clients to arrive unprepared. Like all agendas, it defines the parameters of your time and topics with all kinds of meta messages. It reduces uncertainty on the client's part. It shows you are organized and that you value both your time and the client's time. It reinforces that you are in control of your practice and their account. It raises the bar on the professional tone and the expectation of the meeting. It's one more little indicator that you are worth it.

When scheduling meetings, keep in mind the restraints and benefits of the calendar year. Meetings in the run-up to Christmas or during summer holiday season can be a write-off for clients. Similarly, tax and RSP seasons can be a write-off for you.

You may have rolled your eyes earlier when I described my adventure at the hair salon. Well, that salon is a multi-million dollar business; every time someone walks in, they leave about $300 for whatever gorgeousness they bought. Those clients don't walk in off the street; they have scheduled appointments. So let me underscore this: if a hair appointment is important enough to merit a pre-booked time, then your money is too. Without question.

And if your clients or prospective clients don't agree, then this is an opportunity, not an obstacle. They have probably never worked with a professional VSA before. Just think of how awesome your relationship is going to be for them.

PLUGGING CORE ACTIVITIES INTO YOUR PROCESS

So your clients now have a series of meetings booked with you, and you have planned to send out statements, financial articles and non-financial information to your clients between these meetings to stay in touch. In addition, you are also going to call them every ninety days to say hello and make sure you are aware of any recent events in their lives.

When are each of these activities supposed to take place? Who will call to confirm the meeting? How many days prior will that call be placed? What will the caller say when they call? Are you going to leave that up to the person making the call or, as the owner of your practice, are you going to ensure that it is scripted? Who will print the agenda, and will it be mailed, couriered or emailed? What about your call rotation? A client call is an important event. You may wish that it contain key messages, both overt and implied. Just as you follow an outline or script for your meetings, we advise the same with call rotations.

RECAP

In formulating your Experience Matrix, each of your clients, regardless of the tier they are in as determined by your client segmentation, receives the same core financial services: an annual meeting, regular financial reports, quarterly telephone CLAN calls, articles of interest.

Your best clients receive more frequent meetings and client events. In addition, you trawl the Internet and periodicals to send them articles of non-financial interest based on their unique pursuits.

Every member of your team adheres to providing all of your clients with excellent and personal service delivery. If you are already doing all the right things, ask among your team how you all might do them a little better, and then implement.

You constantly look for ways of differentiating your clients' experience with your practice to make it more memorable so that they will notice and talk about you.

Chapter 6

Process: Drink the Pink Goo

MOST ADVISORS' GOALS FOR more profitable, predictable and enjoyable practices are undermined due to their failure to implement processes that drive a consistent experience. Without implementing formal processes that define the structure and operating philosophy of the business, it's difficult, if not impossible, for advisors to measure their current situation and the relative success of new initiatives they undertake to achieve business goals.

Most people don't really know how to formalize a process. We all may have excellent ideas, and we all may be able to identify the process of a great experience we've personally enjoyed, but to actually incorporate a process into one's business is incredibly challenging.

There is good news: once you learn how to implement, you will quickly become a master of not only incorporating processes into your business but also creating new processes that you can measure and adjust. With processes mastered, you will actually work *on* your business versus *in* your business. You will see that you are a business owner first and a financial advisor second.

As Michael Gerber identified in the *E-Myth*, the true shift from "working in your business" to "working on your business," occurs when the business owner creates defined boundaries and definitions for how the business will operate and function.

This is a distinguishing characteristic of VSAs, taking a methodical, focused approach to improving their business. In fact, the majority of their energy is focused on achieving business efficiency, which would not be possible without processes.

One of the most common questions I hear is, "How do I get my team to buy into it?" We have all been a part of campaigns that go nowhere. This may be because they are not well thought out, or they are executed sporadically. More often than not, they miss the mark completely. Everyone feels defeated.

Short-term as well as long-term harm is done when this happens. As an advisor, you lose focus, and your business might stray from what it actually is meant to do. You miss opportunities and waste your resources. Over the long haul, your credibility as a team leader suffers.

The truth is that no one on your team is going to do anything, and results won't pan out until the company and its team embraces the movement. From the top on down – from the CEO/boss to each team member – everyone has to believe in the promise you make to your clients. Everyone has to look at what they do within the enterprise as a function of fulfilling that promise.

Getting your team to buy into the shift to process may be something that is mandated. My thoughts, however, is that when the team is involved in the development of processes, they take ownership, and dictating your new protocols is unnecessary.

There is an often-told story from the NASA space program of the late 1960s. Some particular event was taking place that was receiving national coverage. All the reporters were there because the space race was on, and NASA and all things space could not have been any cooler or hotter, depending on which way you want to measure it. As the reporters were waiting for the start of an important press conference, a janitor happened to come along. One of the reporters, perhaps to have some sport, asked the janitor, "And what do you do here?" Reportedly, the janitor stopped, put his hands on top of the broom handle and said, "I put people on the moon."

I wasn't there so who knows how much of this is urban myth. But I like to believe is that this actually happened and that the janitor was teaching them a lesson. The lesson is that it is not easy to put people on the moon and then return them to earth. There are a lot of steps along the way, a lot of key pieces and key people. Everything has to be followed perfectly and predictably. There isn't any one person involved with the project on any level who doesn't fully commit to their role in it, even if that is making sure that the top scientists and engineers don't slip when they round a corner.

The point of this story is to show how a team must operate to achieve its goals. Some roles within an organization might be more technical or complex than someone else's, but everyone understands how critically important their responsibility is within the process. Each, in his or her own way, contributes. Each, in his or her own way, takes ownership.

The benefits are discernible. Team members, through process, more easily share information and come to rely on one another. They have energy derived from understanding and achieving a common purpose – the fulfillment of the client experience, the fulfillment of the corporate promise and obligation. *Your* obligation.

Teams that are not driven by process are instead driven by raw talent or – as often as not – the lack thereof. I've worked with dozens of advisors over the years who have signed on after years of indecision because their assistant retired or left for greener pastures (probably to work for an advisor who relies on process). However, until the assistant quit, these same advisors were content to carry on as they always had, doing the best they could without a formalized plan because they had a competent person in place to pick up the slack.

Process will set them – and you – free. Remember that scene in the film *The Abyss*, when Ed Harris had to swallow all the liquid pink goo so that he can breathe underwater? He literally had to drown himself to breath. That is what you have to do here – commit. Trust me. Process will liberate you.

Process will also increase your perceived value in the eyes and opinions of your clients. The experience that is delivered through attention to detail, consistency and predictability will underscore greater consideration and professionalism on the part of you and your team.

The primary challenge in running and managing a business is controlling and solving for constraints. Constraints are bottlenecks that cause the business to become ineffective and inefficient. The typical response to a constraint is to try and work harder, faster or more efficiently. These strategies may work for a period, but they never solve the longer-term problem. Every time this cycle repeats itself, the business diverts more and more of its resources inward and becomes increasingly reactive. We all know what that feels like.

The biggest obstacle for a financial advisor when they shift to "working on their business" is having a meaningful and compelling reason to change, being able to accurately identify and solve for constraints, and having effective tools and processes to ensure that they do not get dragged into the day-to-day minutiae of running the business. These three requirements will ensure that your business continues to focus the majority of its resources in a proactive manner:

1. Understanding who does what in your organization.
2. Understanding and defining how things are done.
3. Identifying and solving for constraints.

The advisor who analyzes and continually reviews these aspects of his or her business will, over time, create an efficient and effective practice that consistently and predictably delivers an experience that clients will want to tell others about.

STEP ONE: YOUR ORGANIZATION CHART

The first step to converting your business into one that is more process-driven is to figure out three critical things: who do you have, what do they do, and what do they need to do?

You might be the owner, but that doesn't mean you are the most important person in your business. Yes, the buck stops with you, but you can't be involved with everything that happens in your enterprise. You should only be busy on those activities that make the most sense to you from an expertise, revenue-generation and personal enjoyment standpoint.

In my company, I don't answer the phone. I don't go to Staples, nor do I go to the post office. Once I have written my blog, I don't have anything more to do with it. Technology in the office? I'm not the one taking care of it. I put my holidays and personal events on the calendar, and my assistant schedules everything around them.

I do speak with every prospect. I do host every W5 call. However, the call is the ninth step in a nineteen-step process. It's the talking on the phone that drives the revenue.

By the time I arrive at work, my entire day is laid out for me. I insist on making the coffee because, as everyone around me knows, I make the best coffee known to humankind. Once I turn on my computer, everything I need to know and do that day is right there, and all the people I will speak with are informed and prepared. I am on autopilot from that point until I leave the office. When I get home at night, I've got the emotional and mental energy to play with my kids and enjoy my down time.

Your org chart need not be complex. You can set it up in one of several ways. You may wish to list activities under the category headings of each team member or under the category headings of your primary divisions of service delivery and management. The charts in Figures 1 and 2 (on the next page) illustrate either option.

Next, plug in all the activities that fall under these main categories. You'll need to dig into the details of your operation so that every single activity is documented. For example, someone has to answer the phone. Someone has to send the mail. Someone has to update the webpage. Someone has to ensure that clients are greeted and cared for. Someone has to attend to administration, and someone has to do the portfolios. Someone has to host the review meetings. The list goes on and on.

Figure 1: Org Chart A – Team Members

Advisor	Administrative Assistant	Client Services Manager
Client Experience Matrix Development	Client file organization	Answering the phones
Financial plans	Compliance requirements	Confirming appointments
Centers of Influence	Daily office procedures	

If you have drafted an org chart that uses the template shown in Figure 2, leave space below each item so that the names of those in your office who are responsible for each activity can be assigned. In Figures 1 and 2 shown here, examples of required tasks and assignment to the relevant team member have been provided for illustrative purposes. Modify your org chart according to your own office needs.

Figure 2: Org Chart B – Operational Divisions

Marketing	Sales	Client Experience	Operations	General Management	Administration
Events	Onboarding	Matrix development	Financial Plans	Procedures manual	Client file organization
(Advisor)	*(Advisor/AA)*	*(Advisor)*	*(Advisor)*	*(AA)*	*(AA)*
Centers of Influence	New Client Welcome	Confirming appointments	Compliance Requirements	Daily office procedures	Answering Phones
(Advisor)	*(Advisor/AA)*	*(AA)*	*(AA)*	*(AA)*	*(CM)*

To help you get started, I've listed some areas that each requires a process. This is not a definitive listing; you may not require some items on the list, whereas you may have others that have not been included.

Accounting procedures
Back office
Call rotations
Client Experience Matrix development
Client onboarding process
Client segmentation strategy
Community involvement
Confirming appointments
Daily office procedures
Email protocols
Event and/or workshop management
Financial plans
Greeting clients
Mail and courier procedures
New client welcome process
Procedures and protocols manual
Reporting
Review meetings
Scheduling appointments and calls
Trading/orders
Webpage maintenance

Answering the phones
Business plan reviews
Centers of Influence
Client file organization
Client right-sizing strategy and process
Client transfer/reassignment logistics
Compliance requirements
CRM task automation
Data backups
Equipment Procurement and Maintenance
Filling out product applications
Formatting written communications
Inventory
Networking
Office supplies
Professional development and training
Returning phone messages
Scheduling and preparing for staff meetings
Scheduling vacations and time out of office
Transaction procedures
Weekly Team Meetings

STEP TWO: UNDERSTANDING AND DEFINING PROCESSES

Every single process in your business has to be identified and assigned to help you fulfill your obligation, which is to provide your clients with an experience that will solidify their relationship with you and your team. Now you need to decide upon all the details of the experience that will deliver on that promise.

For example, when welcoming a client to your office, what can you do to "clear away questions and empower clients?" Let's brainstorm a little on the types of questions you need to consider in order to answer that question.

Does sending the agenda for your review meeting ahead of time help clear away questions for your client? Would a call prior to the meeting help set the agenda? Does having a team member meet clients in the lobby promote a more positive experience as opposed to having clients check in with the receptionist who then notifies you? Is it more advantageous to have both individuals in a couple attend your meetings so that you are able to clear away questions and concerns without one having to relate what transpired in the meeting after the fact? And after the meeting, would sending follow-up notes to your client be helpful? What about a follow-up call instead? Will any of your appointment confirmation calls, your review meeting text, your follow-up emails be scripted so that each client receives a consistent experience? And so on.

In the previous chapter, I described the core financial activities that are deliverable to every one of your clients as review meetings and financial planning; reporting; financial/economic client events; additional financial communication; and call rotations. Let's select one and draft up a process template that includes the elements you and your team need to consider when creating the process. In this case, I'll choose the Call Rotation. First, we'll consider the framework of the template:

Figure 3: Process Requirements – Call Rotation

Template Items	Description
Date	Change the date each time the process is altered.
Who	Use the job title of the person responsible for the procedure
Frequency	When is the task to be carried out?
	What factors determine that you should be doing it?
	Is there a regular or recurring frequency when the actions are to be carried out?
Process	List the specific actions which must be done to complete the task.
	Explain these actions in detail. Be sure to include every step necessary.
Scripting	If scripting is required to complete this task, draft the text.
Resources	Identify the letters, forms, scripts that are required to complete this task. Describe where the resources are physically located in the office.

Now we'll look at how this framework can be applied to a Call Rotation:

Figure 4: Template Sample of a 90-day Call Rotation

	90-Day Call Rotation
Date:	(Date of last process amendment)
Who:	Advisor: All Platinum and Gold clients
	Administrative Assistant: Silver clients
Frequency:	Platinum and Gold clients: every 90 days
	Silver clients: every 180 days
Process:	Review client's information in your CRM; note any CLAN information that would be useful during the call.
	Make the call.
	Leave a message if you get voice mail, using the Call Rotation Script.
	If you reach the client, use the Call Rotation Script.
	Update CLAN information upon completing the call.
	Schedule the next call rotation either 90 or 180 days forward, unless automated.
	If any Moment of Truth (an outstanding accomplishment or event) has occurred, schedule to take action on it the next day.
Scripting:	Call Rotation Script
	Call Rotation Message Script
Resources:	CRM
	Client CLAN information

In terms of who on your team should create which process, I suggest that in the areas of delivering upon the client experience, which includes meeting all core financial essentials, client onboarding, new client welcomes, review meetings and client right-sizing, you should be the one responsible. After all, you are the one who made the promise to your clients, and it is your relationship with each of them that will drive your business forward.

Operational, management and marketing processes can be delegated, which you can then review and fine-tune. When assigning these tasks, the following approach may work best:

Ask your team to document their activities over the period of a typical week. They may wish to use a chart that breaks their day into hours. While this may initially seem time-consuming, it will reap huge dividends down the road. Have team members compile their activities into a list. Create a schedule for when delegated processes are due and from whom. Assign a manager to compile all drafted processes and related scripts into a Procedures Manual. This should be an electronic copy that all members can access.

When each member of your team comes to learn who is responsible for fulfilling which activities and when, you will find a reduction in time lost to tasks that have been duplicated or when one staff member has asked another for help. The procedures manual brings clarity to each activity and allows the team to focus their time and energy on activities which truly matter, which are enhancing the client experience.

You might have to revisit each process once or twice; in fact, I hope you do as you work to perfect your experience.

You are on your way, my friend.

CONSTRAINTS: NOT A LOVE STORY

It took until now in this book to finally give my business partner, Tom Frisby, his due.

Tom is my friend and a mentor of sorts. Tom has changed my life for the better and forever, and the best part is he made it seem so easy, almost effortless. It may be that when Tom reads this, he'll have completely different thoughts on the matter. I mean, I *assume* he felt it was easy to get me to embrace process.

Our entire business is process driven. From the moment the lights are turned on in the morning until we shut down and head home at night, absolutely anything that touches a client, that fulfills our promise and obligation, is broken down into scripted and automated steps. Everything.

We study best practices, so we are able to measure our results and quickly make adjustments when required. Little time is wasted chasing our tails, wondering if – or why – the sky is falling. Our blog goes out automatically at a very specific time because we have tracked when our CLAN likes to read it, which is first thing in the morning. Gone are the days when I posted blogs every once in a while, on random days at random times.

The arrival of our daily blogs is now consistent and predictable to our clients. We know this because of the favorable feedback we receive that tells us it is anticipated and expected, usually one of the first three emails our clients receive every morning.

We weren't always so organized. One Monday a while back, Tom and I were deep into our scorecard meeting (which will be covered in the next section on measurement), discussing the sporadic results of our client onboarding process as it related to our private consulting program.

To be frank, our numbers were disappointing and we couldn't understand why, as so many of these failed relationships had started with such promise.

Tom compiled a spreadsheet with the objective of helping us discover the constraint, or bottleneck. It wasn't a complicated procedure, just a simple but incredibly powerful way to make our process visual. Across the top of the spreadsheet were the various steps involved in our onboarding process. Very simple stuff.

Figure 5: DMWSC Constraint Spreadsheet

Suspects	Prospects			Clients
Step 1:	Step 2:	Step 3	Step 4	Step 5
Card Given	Completed Introductory Call	Return of W5 Form	Complete Teleconference Call	Onboard
Suspect A	x	x	x	
Suspect B	x	x	x	x
Suspect C	x	x	x	
Suspect D	x			
Suspect E	x	x	x	
Suspect F	x	x	x	
Suspect G	x	x	x	
Suspect H	x	x	x	
Suspect I	x			
Suspect J	x	x	x	
Suspect K	x	x	x	
Suspect L	x	x	x	x
Suspect M	x	x	x	
Suspect N	x			
Suspect O	x	x	x	
Suspect P	x	x	x	

Listed in the left-hand column were all of the ***Suspects***, and the list was pretty long. Let me just say that to get into the Suspect column, all a person had to do was hand me a card or contact our office via email or a call and tell us they were interested. "That was fantastic," they might have told me when I walked off stage. "How can I work with you?" I would take their card, and voila, they entered our process as a suspect. Little more than "one who breathes" was known about them.

So that was the Suspect column. Listed in the last column at the right were all of our clients who came onboard from that list of suspects. I'm sorry to say that the list on the left-hand side was considerably longer than the one of the right. So why?

Between those two columns, starting from the left, were the sequenced steps in our process, one column per step. The headings of those columns were things like "Completed Introductory Call" and "Return of W5 Form" etc. (Here's the beauty of the observation at this moment: we tracked these things. As you will see, that one fact alone made all we learned possible.) As we scanned from left to right, it was obvious that the list of interested advisors consistently shrank. While this was to be expected – not everyone who is interested is going to become a client – we felt that the drop-off was far too significant.

From the moment a Suspect interacted with our office by either returning our introductory phone call or W5 form, they were now deemed to be ***Prospects.*** The names in these Prospect columns were a little fewer; the list had become a little shorter. As mentioned, to be considered a prospect, one had to return our follow-up call and agree to fill out and return our W5 form as well as book time for a teleconference. Some prospects would evaporate and not fill out the form, but the vast majority were genuinely interested and continued with our process.

The purpose of the teleconference call was to discuss the information shared in the W5 form; it also allowed us to learn a little more about the advisor and their current situation. In turn, we told them a little more about our services.

I want to reiterate that every step in the course of this process was considered and prepared. Email templates had been created and used, telephone scripts were followed to confirm appointments. Everything that we felt was within our control was taken into consideration to ensure that the experience of learning about us and about our services was as enlightening and enjoyable as possible.

Following our process, at the end of the W5 teleconference call, each prospect was asked to take a few days to consider everything they had learned and to consider how committed they were to undertaking this action of change.

There was very little drop-off from the first column to the third column. Obviously, we were doing really well bringing people along from general interest to specific interest and evaluation. Some of the drop-off was of our own doing. Our onboarding process was designed to help us learn about our potential clients as well, to determine if there was alignment between both parties.

We find it completely understandable that we may not be appealing to every potential client. So our process allows for a decision to be made in this regard that saves everyone's time and energy in a pleasant and easy manner.

This brought us to the fourth column, and this is where the problem was. The attrition rate was staggering. The sample spreadsheet above pretty well sums up the actual spreadsheet we were looking at.

Instantly, it was clear that the constraint in our process was Step 4, in which we asked the client to take three days to think it over. Obviously, Step 4 wasn't having the desired effect on our prospects.

They were evaporating.

While the purpose of the three-day consideration period was to ensure that our prospects didn't feel pressure in agreeing to work with us, there was also the reservation on my side not to leave an impression of "closing a sale" only to discover a little later on that we weren't aligned with the client and all the stress that accompanies it. While the thinking behind the process was indeed noble, this outcome was clearly unacceptable.

In a world in which we have the tools to track how many hits our websites get, how many phone calls come into an office and so on, I'd like to point out that very few people would take the time to 1) track the numbers and 2) compile a visual report so that they could uncover and solve the constraint.

Most people treat the symptom and not the underlying issues; subsequently, they direct their resources (time, energy, money) at the wrong solutions. "We are not bringing enough new clients onboard," they tell themselves. "Maybe it's because we are charging too much. Maybe there isn't enough perceived value in our service, so we should offer to do more, put more time in. Maybe we need to add another staff member and have that person follow up with all the suspects and prospects who flamed out."

We were no different. We considered each of these possibilities and a few more along with them. But it was Tom who was smart enough to convert the process into a visual chronology that pinpointed where the process had become constrained.

Had he not done this, I'm certain that we would have eventually figured it out but not before we first wasted a lot of time, money and energy. Those resources are finite, and while we will all make some mistakes and waste some resources, these types of responses can become critical.

We usually reference the positive benefits of process: increased revenues and a greater sense of control of your time. But there is also a benefit to process when things are not going well. Processes are measurable, and they allow you to identify a constraint and solve the issue in minutes. No mystery. No hunting, no seat of your pants adjusting. Just measurement.

We eliminated step four, and the next three prospects became clients effortlessly.

All of a sudden, we were transformed from entrepreneurs with good ideas to entrepreneurs with good ideas and certainty. We had found and fixed our problem, the business made some profit, and we lived to fight another day.

I was liberated, amigo. Trust me, drink the pink goo.

Figure 6: How to use a Constraint Matrix

Step 1: Identify a Constraint (bottleneck)	• Look for areas where work flows get hung up or slowed, where team members get frustrated or overwhelmed or where your ability to implement client service is substandard. • The constraint may be a person, process or technology.
Step 2: Describe the Constraint	• How does it look? • When does it happen? • Is it caused by a lack of training? • Does having a flawed process in place cause it? • Are you maximizing the use of your technology? • Do you need new technology?
Step 3: Identify Possible Solutions	• What are the options for solving the constraint? • What resources are available to assist you? • The more options the better!
Step 4: Choose a Solution	• Weigh the options from Step 3 and select the strategy that will maximize the result of solving the constraint.
Step 5: Action Required	• What are the action steps to implement the solution? • Organize them sequentially into a realistic action plan.
Step 6: Monitoring Change	• Any implementation requires accountability. • Establish the timeline for implementation, and put these times on your weekly team meeting agenda to ensure you and your team are accountable for making these important changes.

MEASUREMENT

The sooner you discover constraints and correct them, the sooner you achieve your goals. How much time you choose to spend floundering for answers is entirely up to you. Without process, what can you measure?

Let's go back to the above example where my company was not bringing on as many private consulting clients as we desired. What if we didn't have process? How – and how quickly – would we have found the constraint and solved it? What would we have measured? The bottom line? If we had measured the bottom line, all we would have discovered was there wasn't enough bottom to the line. Now what? What would that have told us?

It would have told us next to nothing. Would knowing we didn't make *enough* money have told us how to make *more* money? Nope.

The steps of a process are the only variables that you can actually measure. The bottom line is the result of the process. A healthy bottom line suggests a dialed-in process; a lousy bottom line suggests a process that is non-existent or one in need of some work. In our case, we were able to measure a process and identify the constraint at Step Four, and as a result, we experienced our best year in terms of revenue, relaxation and ease.

Without a process, you measure by proxy. Because one can't measure anything concrete, a substitute is instead chosen. In most cases, that substitute is based on a feeling.

For example, let's say I have forty suspects interested in becoming private consulting clients, but I have no formal process. I show my partner Tom the forty cards and say, "I bet we have six clients in there." I am measuring a feeling based on an assumption about the likelihood of a suspect becoming a client based on the enthusiasm I had detected in that person's voice. Maybe I am right, or maybe I am wrong. But you would have to agree with me that my conclusion is simply a guess. I would be measuring nothing and assuming everything.

There are billions of dollars spent every year in the weight loss industry. These fads, plans and programs come and go. One of them, Weight Watchers, has been around for a very long time. There's a reason. Something about the Weight Watchers' program sets it apart from the other programs.

If you've ever been on this program, you'll know what it is right away: measurement and accountability. You have to write down everything that you eat, convert it to whatever their latest measurement tool is, whether that's food group portions, points or calories, and then let yourself be weighed in front of one of their attendants. It's like going to Confession. You have to inspect what you expect.

Tom and I have two weekly meetings. Tom and our assistant, Nick, have a weekly meeting, and Nick and I have our own meetings every week. Sometimes, out of necessity the meeting has to be rescheduled, but we never allow ourselves to drift more than two weeks.

Every week, Tom and I have a "scorecard meeting" where we discuss and track all of our opportunities. We are doing two things: we are measuring real data, and we are qualifying our opportunities. "You were going to call ABC Inc. and speak to the National Sales Manager about doing some work with them. What did you do? What happens next? When is the next action due?"

We do this every single week. Opportunities either convert to clients, or they flame out. New opportunities appear, and we determine the potential of these new opportunities, set goals for commitment and so on.

A weekly team meeting is an efficient and effective method to ensure everyone on your team understands the common goals and activities of your business for the coming week, month and year. It provides a structured forum for reinforcing new business practices, fostering a proactive business model, preventing 'slippage', which are those things that fall through the cracks, and bringing order and focus to your team.

THE WEEKLY TEAM MEETING

The weekly team meeting will allow you and your team to experience the following:

- Minimized interruptions throughout week, allowing everyone to be more focused and on task.

- Clearly outlined client-specific deliverables for the week, ensuring a proactive approach (ie. all necessary preparations are done ahead of time) that keeps everyone on the same page.
- Reports on the status of 'new' and 'existing' client transfers.
- A venue for monthly progress reporting of new clients, new assets and average account size.
- A structured forum for sharing and recording of client-specific information such as birthdays, CLAN and other information such as upcoming client holidays, etc.
- Focus on business development projects: monitoring their status from inception through to completion.
- Amendments and additions to process protocols for updating in the Procedures manual.
- Full awareness of upcoming staff training, holidays or other issues that may affect the day-to-day operations of the business.

Conducting team meetings on a weekly basis rather than less frequently serves several purposes. Team members will spend less time interrupting each other during the course of their workdays to deal with specific situations if they know it can be addressed as a group within the week. Meetings will be shorter and more proactive when they happen regularly and frequently. Obstacles, challenges, problems – however you wish to phrase them – can be remedied more quickly and efficiently because there is less history to backtrack. Team member autonomy and team member harmony and awareness of each other's importance are further fostered. Add as you will to this list.

Choose a weekly day and time to meet that is convenient to everyone. The beginning of the week tends to work well for many advisors and their staff. Fridays, on the other hand, are generally not recommended due to days off, early departures, other meetings and the like.

Book the team meeting into everyone's organizer as a reoccurring weekly commitment. Do not skip the meeting due to one team member's absence unless you are a team of two because, in addition to hampering the benefits listed in the paragraph above, it implies that the whole is less important that the part that is missing. That is never true. Instead, forward the missing member the notes of the meeting so that they can catch up.

Use a Weekly Team Meeting Agenda to ensure your meetings are efficient and effective. Agendas help keep everyone on task and allow members to share all that needs to be communicated within the team in a timely manner. Use a basic template for every meeting. Post the agenda in your database and invite team members to add items they wish to address. This will allow the meeting facilitator to know in advance the time the meeting will consume and to set limits accordingly. Assign a meeting facilitator who adheres to the agenda and moves things along. At the outset of the meeting, make sure everyone has a copy of the agenda with the new items included.

Meetings shouldn't take more than thirty minutes. Attempt not to put off any items to the next meeting unless everyone agrees that, due to the economies of time, a matter can be deferred.

Each attendee must be up-to-date with respect to the areas of business operations they are responsible for. Consistency will be important in forming and reinforcing your new structured approach to team communication.

RECAP

Processes are structures; they serve your practice in fundamental ways. They enable you and your team to deliver to new and existing clients a customized and unique experience that solidifies your relationship with them and promotes business growth. They enable you to diagnose constraints and measure performance. They streamline the day-to-day, month-to-month and year-over-year efficiencies of office management.

Lack of process wears people down, whereas process provides comfort and reassurance. Relying on established processes will allow you to shift your time, energy and money resources outward so that all members of the team can be as proactive as possible in creating an excellent client experience.

Implementing processes grows out of the plan you have created that segments clients by the benefits they bring to your practice, whether those benefits are assets under management, fees or referrals. The first step in creating these processes is to identify who within your organization does what. Once those divisions of labor and responsibility have been identified, they are converted into detailed work flows that include supporting documentation and resources. These work flows are communicated among team members through a procedures manual and weekly team meetings.

Constraints to your business need to be remediated through the analysis of process and performance metrics in order to ensure that experience delivery is continually improved.

Chapter 7

The Four Key Processes of Rebranding

YOU'RE NOW SOLD ON THE idea that processes will shape your business into something new and exciting: an organization with efficiency, predictability, measurement, structure and excellence. Your team is on board with the whole idea of shifting from a sales and marketing business model to one of experience delivery. Everyone is invigorated, documenting how their time is spent, identifying constraints, generating ideas on how to work around them, mapping out how best to bring superior value to your clients. Everybody is pumped.

But they are still looking to you for solutions. You are, after all, their fearless leader, the one from whom all this brilliance has flowed.

And you know what is needed. You know that you need to grow your business through referrals from your best clients because the odds are very favorable that they will bring you clients just like themselves. You know that you need to ally with other professionals who will endorse your services to their best clients and that you will repay in kind. You know this will take time and energy, but you are patient because good things come to those who work hard and let momentum build.

Keep in mind that the following four key processes that will transform your practice take place simultaneously, and the order in which they are presented by no means needs to be the order in which you implement. Because you are now in the experience business, they are all directed at achieving a common goal: to create a sustainable alignment of mutual respect, trust and shared purpose between you and each of your clients.

PROCESS ONE: RIGHT-SIZING

Regardless of the size of your business, one thing is probably true: you have just the right number of team members to meet current demand. You're certainly not carrying staff who are twiddling their thumbs. If anything, the opposite may be true. You may actually be finding yourself neck deep in activity, only too aware of that old bromide, the one telling you not to confuse activity for productivity. You know all that, but you might still be too mired in the bustle of your current routine to do very much about it. The phones still keep ringing non-stop, fires still pop up and need drenching, your work hours still exceed what you'd like to put in, and all of this because a dollar still needs to be earned. Something has got to give.

So we're back to needing to define boundaries around the expenditure of time and energy so that everyone on your team can devote more of both implementing the new processes you want to create. Still, it's a question of where do you find the time?

It's always nice to hear from clients, especially when they have good things to tell us. We all love those kinds of phone calls. We love them even more when our clients have the names of other folks they'd like us to follow up with. Those kinds of phone calls let us know we are doing a great job, and they give us the opportunity to grow our business in exactly the ways we want it to grow.

Every advisory practice has clients they hear from. Sometimes, more often than they'd like, these practices also have clients they hear from incessantly. And often – not always, but often enough – these clients are not the ones with sizable portfolios.

I don't want to disparage these clients whose assets under management aren't very large. They are doing the right thing by saving for a rainy day, putting away for retirement, investing. They are good people, even if they sometimes phone us a lot.

They may have been brought on board in the days when you were building your practice, when all comers were welcomed with open arms. They may be the friends or family members of really important clients whose business and whose relationships mean a lot to you. There are probably as many reasons for why you have these clients as there are clients. It doesn't matter. Now that you've segmented your clients by portfolio size and determined where your revenues are really coming from, you need to look at the clients in the lowest echelons of assets under administration closely.

Let's look once more at our Client Segmentation chart from Chapter 4, specifically at that bottom tier of Silver clients:

Figure 1: Client Segmentation Tiers

Level	Tier	Client Attributes
Platinum	Tier 1	• Refer regularly (at least once a year for the past number of years) • In the top 50% of revenue • Meet your alignment criteria
Platinum	Tier 2	• In the top 50% of revenue • Meet alignment criteria
Platinum	Tier 3	• In the top 50% of revenue • Not fully aligned • May have one or more red flags • They are your client because of the income you generate from them
Gold	Tier 4	• 35% of revenue • Meet your alignment criteria • May or may not refer • Level 2 without the assets/revenue
Silver	Tier 5	• The bottom 15% of revenue • Anyone from Tier 3 or 4 who is not a fit for your business

For many of your bottom-tier clients, it's time to part ways.

I know that for many of you, the realization that you might not be able to keep all of your clients can cause discomfort. Somehow, the whole notion seems anti-business, against everything you've believed has brought you to where you are right now. And during your growth phase, that approach to business-building served you well.

However Silver, or Tier 5, clients generate 15% of our imaginary practice. They do not refer. They are not aligned with our objectives or Ideal Client profile. They do not take much of our time; they receive one meeting a year and their monthly statements. If they were at the Oscars, they would be the seat fillers.

Now consider them from the perspective of the following anecdote.

In the course of our consulting and coaching activities with our advisory clients, we asked several office teams to track the classifications of inbound client phone calls according to the tier levels in Figure 1.

Their discoveries were startling to everyone concerned: fully 70% of inbound calls were from clients in Tiers 4 and 5. Furthermore, 40% of those calls were from clients in the lowest tier. To drive the point home, phone calls from Tier 5 clients were consuming 28% of all inbound calls yet generating only 15% of these firms' revenues. The next question is obvious: what might be the impact if the service hours that this percentage consumed were instead devoted to providing additional experiences to the highest revenue-generating group, the one poised to refer new business from people like themselves? Would the loss of revenue from the lowest tier be recovered by referrals from the higher tiers?

That is a rhetorical question, in case you felt inclined to answer it. Of course the revenue would be recovered. And in the case of our coaching clients, it in fact was.

You cannot afford to have such a large amount of valuable time and energy being consumed by a relatively unprofitable segment of your business. In your quest to free your personal resources as well as those of your team, you need to divest yourself of clients whose business isn't really business at all.

To commence your process of right-sizing, you need to keep in mind that it must be done professionally and progressively so that the impact of revenue loss is mitigated by that of revenue growth at the top end of your client segmentation. In order to do that, I suggest you do the following:

Create a master list of all Tier 5 clients, ordering the list from highest account size to lowest.

Identify where or to whom each Tier 5 client will be reassigned. Meet with advisors within your network who are actively growing their assets and would be agreeable to take on these clients. It may be that your firm has a 1-800 service that would be suitable for some of these clients.

Select a group of clients from the bottom of your Tier 5 list.

Send the clients in this group a reassignment letter. In the letter, explain that you have made changes to your practice that relate to your overall approach to wealth management and financial planning, and that the impact of these changes have lead you to conclude that you can no longer serve their best interests. Let them know you have transferred their account to a new advisor who will be calling them shortly to set up a meeting so that there is no interruption to the service they receive, and include a copy of the new advisor's biography and business card. End by thanking them for their trust and confidence over the years.

In six months, assess the new assets or annual revenue that have been added to your business, and reassign the next lowest group of Tier 5 clients that equals the new business that was added to your book.

As you can see, systematically right-sizing your practice over time will minimize the impact upon your revenues.

But in other ways – positive ways – this impact can be profound. One corporate client with whom we worked realized the following in only the first sixteen months of right-sizing:

- Divested 242 clients (44% of households) with $14M in total assets (9% of total assets under administration) which had generated $140,000 (9% of total fees) in fees per annum.
- Gained 16 new client relationships with 12M in assets and $120,000 in fees per annum.

- Gained back, on average, 2 hours of time in each team member's workday to streamline office management and devote to servicing their remaining higher-revenue generating clients and client referrals.
- Reduced the advisor's work week to 40 hours from 50.

In an earlier chapter, I talked about measurement and how important it is to track your progress and uncover constraints. Similarly, measure revenue losses and gains during your right-sizing process. The following table can be modified so that you're able to monitor these changes to your revenues/assets.

You may receive a few phone calls from clients being redirected, expressing the desire to stay with you. A few of them may even make a strong case, and if you feel that they are aligned with your purposes, deal with these calls as you see fit. Keep in mind your objectives, however: you need to gain time and energy and serve only those clients who will bring you more business, whether in assets, revenues or referrals. There is absolutely no room for dead weight.

Figure 2: Financial Size-Up

	Last Year	Year 2	Year 3	Year 4	Year 5
Retention rate as a % Departed assets / Total AUM at end of previous year					
Assets per client Total AUM as of Dec. 31 / Total # of clients as of Dec. 31					
Operating Efficiency as a % Annual Net Income / Annual Gross Income					
Sales Growth as a % (Total Sales from previous year minus Total sales in present year) / Total previous year's sales					

PROCESS TWO: REBOOTING YOUR REMAINING CLIENTS

reboot: (*ree-**boot***)
verb (used with object)
1. to shut down and restart

Now that you've started the process of introducing your lowest tier clients to the changes afoot in your practice, it's time to bring your remaining clients up to speed. This is done in person during their next scheduled review meeting, one that takes on special significance (and a new name) for you and your team: the Reboot Meeting. This one-meeting process focuses entirely on resetting and updating the framework of your relationships with existing clients in Tiers 1, 2, 3 and 4.

One of the reasons you are holding Reboot Meetings is to assess the current alignment of your client relationship so that you may begin to deliver – or continue to deliver – a consistent and superior experience to your clients every time you or your office interacts with them. Because you are making changes to the way you work with these existing clients, this meeting will introduce the new way things will be done.

I'm sympathetic to the fact that many advisors feel uncomfortable about reframing the nature of their existing relationships with their best clients, especially those they've enjoyed working with for many years. They worry that the very need to have a Reboot meeting somewhat admits their own lack of expertise and professionalism. They fear that they may come across as showing that they've allowed something that's wrong to be that way for the duration of the relationship.

This simply isn't true. And your clients will understand this when you present it to them in a professionally positive manner. You are going to let your clients know that you have achieved success because of your commitment to take a holistic approach to financial planning, and that over the years, your consistency and personal touch has resulted in your practice growing through word-of-mouth endorsements. You will introduce them to the new approach you are formalizing at your practice, and you want to ensure that it aligns with them because of your desire to keep them as a client.

You are rebranding, just as Target or UPS have or like Old Spice did with that guy on the horse. Your message is positive because the future is positive – for you and for them.

Through the Reboot Meeting, you want to close any gap that has developed between what you think you do for your clients and how they perceive what you do, or can do, for them. Any number of reasons can contribute to this gap – industry changes, changes at your firm, changes in your business and even personal changes, but they represent inconsistencies in past practices. Simply put, the longer someone has been your client, the greater the likelihood that they may not know about your full services. Unless you have been regularly updating, their perception of who you are and what you do has been frozen at the moment they became your client.

Not being fully aligned and current with existing clients is a huge detriment to your business. You may miss important milestones in their lives. You may not realize that another advisor is making recommendations that are contrary to your position. You may not see natural sales opportunities which fit their needs. What would you expect your clients to say to a friend about your practice if your clients are not fully aligned or informed about all the services you provide? How can they accurately describe you to others and make referrals?

The Reboot Meeting lets you stay current with your clients' entire financial situations, to learn more about their personal goals. And it allows you to inform them of your referral process, which is now your most important business-building strategy. In fact, once you've rebooted a client, you should do it at least once a year so that your objectives during the meeting are continually reinforced.

Let's take a look at what those objectives are.

Create scarcity.

By informing your clients that you desire to work with fewer and more specific clients, you reinforce the value you are placing on your relationship with them, and the value you place on the time and talents of your practice. Furthermore, consumer behavior studies support the notion that belonging to a select group is an important factor in where and with whom one does business. It's nice to be considered an Ideal Client.

Reinforce your experience-delivery process.

Explaining to your clients the importance of your processes – how meetings will be conducted, how communications with your office should take place, how referrals are welcomed and dealt with – allows you to close that perception gap I referred to earlier. Your clients need to know about the changes you have implemented, and nothing shows them more clearly than how you conduct the Reboot Meeting.

Bolster your personal and professional integrity.

The manner in which you stress to your client the reasons behind your choice of firm and what the firm offers you professionally underscores your integrity as an advisor. When you add a clear explanation of the type of client who is best suited to your services, you underscore it even more.

We've decided that all of your clients need a Reboot Meeting, that the first one will take place during their next scheduled review meeting, and that it will be repeated as part of your annual service. If you already have a review meeting process that has populated your calendar with client appointments, it's best to stay with that. After all, predictability is one the experiences you have committed your practice to delivering upon.

However, if you are preparing to schedule your first round of Reboot Meetings, keep the following targets in mind

1. Identify your *most important* clients in Tiers 1, 2, 3 and 4. Get to these clients first because they are the individuals whom you cannot

afford to lose nor risk not having fully embrace or understand your unique approach and value. (You might wish to select a few clients from Tiers 3 and 4 for dress rehearsal Reboot Meetings until you become comfortable with your presentation.)

2. Determine which clients hold assets at other firms. Part of your message during the Reboot Meeting, which we'll get into, will address this issue.
3. Identify those clients with whom you get along very well, with whom you feel you have a trusting relationship, and who value your integrity and approach but do not refer new business. It's important that these clients learn of your referral process as soon as possible.
4. Determine whether you are working with COIs (including attorneys, accountants or other related financial professionals) who have referred business to you. The message that you will impart to clients in the Reboot Meeting is one that you will deliver to this network as well, which I'll cover in the next chapter. Leave time in your calendar now to meet with these individuals.

THE NUTS AND BOLTS OF THE REBOOT MEETING

In their pivotal business book, *The Experience Economy*, authors B. Joseph Pine II and James H. Gilmore compare the delivery of a client experience to the staging of a theatrical play.[6] There are props, there are scripts, there is presentation and delivery, there is a stage and scenery upon it. Some of you may be thinking that this all sounds incredibly artificial and disingenuous. It is anything but. Staging and scripting an experience are simply the means by which it becomes predictable, anticipated, expertly executed and totally engaging for your clients. And like the actor who knows his lines, you will become totally prepared and comfortable with what you have to say.

---

[6] B. Joseph Pine II and James H. Gilmore, *The Experience Economy*, (Boston: Harvard Business Review Press, 2011).

Staging

In Chapter 5, I mentioned the importance of staging your meeting experiences, but it bears repeating here so that you have an appreciation for the experience flow from start to finish.

After your assistant has scheduled the meeting but before the scheduled meeting takes place, either mail or courier what is essentially your Introduction package, one you would send to every prospective client. In it, include the meeting agenda, a cover letter, a list of any documents you wish the client to bring, your corporate brochure and testimonial information. If your brochure doesn't include biographies and photographs of you and your team, include those as well. Finally, slip in a nice handwritten card that expresses how you're looking forward to meeting with the client.

Generally speaking, the further away you greet someone from your place of business, the more impressive the experience is for the client. I'm not saying you should be sending a chauffeured town car to pick them up, but having your assistant meet them in the lobby as opposed to having clients check in at reception is a nice point of differentiation. Everything about every experience you deliver has to set you apart from your competitors, and this is simply one means of doing it.

Wherever you choose to host your meeting (your office, the boardroom, or off-site), err on the side of comfort and taste, and be consistent. Consider your props: linens, glassware, snacks and beverages, dietary modifications that address a client's particular needs (gluten-free, lactose-free etc.). When you show that you are paying attention to their individual needs, they fill in the blanks, immediately determining that you are paying this degree of attention to every aspect of their financial needs as well.

Have copies of the Reboot Meeting agenda – the one you sent ahead of time – printed and waiting on the desk or table where the client will sit. In essence, the agenda should be:

1. Meeting Overview
2. Client Update [CLAN information]
3. State of the Nation [financial market review]

4. Enhancing Your Experience
    - The Firm
    - Compensation
    - Our Process
5. Financial Review
    - Goals and Objectives
    - Financial Inventory Update
    - Portfolio Review/Volatility Questionnaire
    - Recommendations/Plans

For your part, have any documentation that will be needed in the meeting, such as the Financial Inventory or your meeting notes, ready as well, even if your assistant will be the one to oversee its completion.

Scripting

You've hosted hundreds if not thousands of review meetings over the course of your career so I'll forego the details of greeting your clients and making them comfortable. Your objective will be slightly different with each client. You may be meeting with a client whom you know has significant additional assets held elsewhere. Or you may be meeting with a client who has completely empowered you as their advisor and with whom you feel a certain measure of friendship, but this client has never referred any new business. Perhaps, in this case, your objective is just to ensure there are no hidden obstacles or hot spots in your relationship, and to have an opportunity to remind the client of your ideal client profile and specific introduction process.

Bearing in mind all these varying purposes, let's break the Reboot Meeting down into its flow so that you have an idea of what to say and why you say it. Note the language in the following examples. I've tried to be mindful of the advice William Strunk Jr. and E.B. White gave in their principles of the English language classic, *The Elements of Style*[7]: "Use definite, specific, concrete language."

---

[7] William Strunk Jr. and E.B. White, *The Elements of Style*, (Ithaca, NY: W.P. Humphrey, 1918).

Suffice to say, you enter the meeting having reviewed your client's CLAN information so that you can use it as a launch pad to engage your client as the meeting begins and to update your notes as the conversation unfolds.

- **C**areer
- **L**ong-term (any long-term plans or milestones reached)
- **A**ctivities (interests, activities, new events)
- **N**ext of kin (kids, parents, future expenses)
- Upcoming events (medical, travel, home improvement?)
- Questions

Next up is a summary of the where the market has been since you last met. This is your chance to manage your client's expectations against the backdrop of the economy, political forces, the financial services industry – arenas in which there is little that the client can control. This is a good time for delivering key messages that support your underlying planning philosophy. For example, it may be that their portfolio has continued to outperform a specific index.

Script: *"Last year, even given the performance of the markets, we did not deal with nearly as much turbulence as other advisors experienced."*

Message: You are with an experienced advisor whose financial acumen is protecting your investments. Other advisors aren't so skilled.

Following the year in review, you've now arrived at the moment of reboot where you introduce your client to your new process and how it will benefit them.

Script: *"We strive at all times, in everything we do to [deliver peace of mind, etc. – insert your own Alignment Statement]. I take a very different approach to working with my clients, and I see my role a little differently than what I feel the typical advisor does. We manage our clients' entire portfolios, coordinating all of their critical financial planning decisions."*

Message: If you have assets elsewhere, I need to know about them, and they should be under my care. This makes me different than other advisors as well.

Script: *"I am building my practice with a smaller number of clients whom I enjoy working with. It is not my desire to be all things to all people; instead I want to focus on being able to meet every need that my clients have."*

Message: You are a select member of an exclusive group, and I am dedicated to taking care of all of your financial matters.

Script: *"I consider myself a Personal Chief Financial Officer (CFO), and I only work for a handful of clients and their families. These clients, similar to yourself, empower me as their primary financial advisor, and I help them navigate all aspects of their financial planning – the obvious ones, like financial and retirement income planning, but also some additional services as well, such as [offer a list]. My goal is to work with people, not accounts. I want to be a trusted resource for you, and I want to help shepherd your portfolio along the way."*

Messages: Here are all the services that I can provide for you. Again, you are a select member of an exclusive group. You are important to me, and I want to be just as important to you. You need to trust me with all of your financial holdings and tell me about all of your financial activities so that I can make the best decisions for your future.

You may now want to review with your client how you are compensated. This is your call, but my belief is that transparency on this matter removes any questions the client may have about your motives surrounding recommendations you make about investments. Financial planners are paid in a variety of ways, each with its own merits. In the following script, I've chosen a fee-based presentation.

Script: *"As you know, we advocate client-focused solutions regardless of compensation or business model. I am a fee-based advisor, which means everything I do for you is bundled into a single fee. I charge [x%] on your total assets to manage, research, report and plan for you. This [x%] pays me, pays the firm, and pays my staff.*

"This approach ensures that you are getting constant attention and that your investments are being professionally managed. We are not looking to catch the latest wave of popular investments. Instead, we are looking to match your tolerance for volatility with well-run investments that will stand the test of time, through good and bad.

"This approach also ensures you sleep at night and allows us to be proactive in our approach as opposed to reactive. In my experience, reactive investment decisions result in more long-term pain than the short-term discomfort of investment volatility."

Message: There should be no secrets between us. The way I'm reimbursed ensures your peace of mind. In return, I ask for full disclosure from you as well. In addition, I'm not a product pusher. I recommend based on your tolerance of risk, and I recommend solid, long-term investments that will build for you over time because your future financial security is important to me.

You're now at the point in your meeting where you address the issue of assets the client may have invested elsewhere.

Script: *"I'd like to explain to you my thoughts on investments you may hold outside of my care, and why it may be more prudent if that were to change. In the past, I've avoided bringing this matter up with you because I didn't want you to feel pressured. Nor did I want to come across as being sales-motivated. It's never a good idea to spread your assets around. However, a lot of investors confuse the saying "don't put all your eggs in one basket" – which really means don't just own a single stock but diversify – with the belief that they should not trust all of their money to one person's advice.*

"In a perfect scenario, every person would have a personal CFO, not a group of advisors. If you, as the CEO of the company called [Client's last name] Inc., needed to make a decision on whether you and your spouse should renovate your home or instead sell it, I would want you to feel comfortable enough to call me for some guidance on the matter so that I could work the numbers and get back to you with a solution.

"When an investor has half their money here and half spread elsewhere, then I cannot say, to the degree that is satisfies me, that I am doing my job correctly. I know what my part of your portfolio is doing, but I have no idea what the other part or parts of your portfolio are doing. Here is why that can be problematic: if I feel bullish on a stock you are holding with me and make moves to increase your allocation, another advisor you are with may feel exactly the same way and do the same thing. As a result, you may have just become over-exposed, but neither of us, as your advisors, knows that. Suddenly, all of your eggs are indeed in one basket, and you would be paying two advisors to make this mistake.

> *"The only solution that makes any sense – and the only solution that I can accept as a professional – is that you have to consolidate your assets with a single advisor whom you trust, whose processes and approach make sense to you, and whom you find working with comfortable. Believe me, I am not trying to strong-arm you. You are one of my favorite clients. I am in fact living up to my end of the bargain which is to operate with integrity, honesty and always in your best interest."*

I don't have to provide an explanation of what this message tells your client about the value of your position on having all of their investments under your care. The reasons are clear, as is your high regard for them as a client and your worth as their advisor.

It's up to you whether you choose to carry only clients whose entire portfolios are under your care. For the reasons provided in the above example and for the streamlining of your business, my advice is that you do. A homogenous clientele enables you to deliver experiences in a more cost-efficient and energy-conserving manner, and whole portfolio management may become one of your criteria for taking on new clients and maintaining existing ones. With that in mind, the segue to this position would be as follows:

Script: *"So this is where I am at. Right now, I have a capacity issue that I fear is going to erode my ability to deliver a superior, Personal CFO experience. As a result, I am moving to a more exclusive practice where I work only with serious investors who value my advice and process and who appreciate the benefits of having a Personal CFO in their corner. Because I will be working with fewer clients, I am able to streamline and customize the delivery of my services. Basically every client I have is so similar that it will become easier for me to take care of them, but it will also ensure a more enjoyable, seamless client experience.*

If all of these changes make sense to you – and I hope they do – we'll continue working together."

Message: It is now time to commit to me as your exclusive advisor. I believe I can provide you with a superior service experience, one I only offer to a select group, and the price for receiving that service is care of all of your investment holdings. You will gain a personal CFO and join an exclusive practice committed to providing you with the highest level of service.

At this point, your clients are beginning to understand by way of example this new experience process you've been referring to.

1. They received an Introduction package as promised to them when your assistant booked their review meeting, one that reintroduced your company, its services, and how the meeting would run.
2. They were personally met by your assistant and accompanied to your office.
3. The meeting started on time, as promised.
4. The meeting environment was comfortable, professional, and tasteful.
5. The agenda is being followed, as promised.
6. You've shown that you pay attention to what's important in the client's life (CLAN) over and above their financial investments.
7. You've underscored the client's value and specialness by wishing to include them in your rebranded, right-sized business.
8. You've taken a position on the importance of holding all of their assets as a criterion for staying with you.

The next part of your new process review transitions logically into describing your Ideal Client (ie. the client currently in front of you) and how you would like your client to refer others to your practice.

PROCESS THREE: ENHANCING THE REFERRAL PROCESS

The essence of garnering referrals is by *being* referable.

Some people will tell you that simply asking for referrals is the key to getting more of them. This is not entirely true. In fact, if the proper foundation has not been laid in advance, asking for referrals can be an exercise in futility. So how can you create a steady referral stream?

The traditional methods of 'asking' for referrals are typically designed to elicit an immediate response from an unsuspecting client. However, asking makes you appear subservient and needy to your client, which generally is not well-received. For these reasons, regular communication about your referral process is a much more professional and courteous way of educating your clients about how you and your team deal with referrals.

It is important that you make the distinction between asking for a referral and offering someone the opportunity to refer a friend or family member to you for help.

When you offer a service that a client can act on independently, you are not imposing on the client. Positioning your referral process so that your clients feel they are helping someone else is something they can appreciate. By framing your referral process as a service to others, you break down the barriers that often impede clients from making a referral on your behalf. Your clients will more likely refer you if they believe they are doing their friends and family members a valuable service rather than just helping you grow your business.

In order for a referral to happen, your clients must be talking about you to others. After a moment of self-reflection, we can accept that we only talk to others about an experience that is either excellent and surpasses our expectations or falls below our expectations. People never talk about the middle ground. You can assume that if you look at your own experiences this way, then your clients likely behave in the same manner. So the basic question becomes: are you building experiences for your clients to enjoy that will surpass their expectations?

Ensuring that your client experience surpasses expectations is an advantage in a highly competitive environment. It allows you to differentiate your value from competitors. This is a critical point, since your clients are being exposed to messages from other financial professionals and are hearing about other financial advisors through family and friends. Therefore, the investment of time, energy and money is well worth the benefit of competitor-proofing your clients so that they have a reason to talk about you.

Communicate Constantly

Once your clients are impressed with the level of service you provide, your next responsibility is to ensure that they don't forget about you. The old adage 'out of sight, out of mind' is certainly true when it comes to getting referrals. If you make it a point to constantly stay in front of your clients, they will always keep you in mind. This way, when their neighbor is complaining that he never hears from his advisor, your client will be quick to say, "You should talk to mine. I hear from him all the time."

If you are looking to build more opportunities for client interaction in your experience processes, here are some effective ways:

- Weekly Market Update by e-mail
- Monthly Wine Tastings
- Annual State of the Markets Workshop
- Mid-Year Market Update Workshop
- Quarterly letter
- Account reviews
- Quarterly call rotations from you and your staff

Host Effective Client Events

Once you have happy clients who hear from you all the time, your referral pond will start to get stocked. One way to capture them is by hosting effective client events. Effective client events share five basic elements:

1. They are either entertaining or educational in nature. Everyone who attends benefits in some way.

2. They vary in subject matter. You want different clients and prospects to attend different events rather than having the same group every time. They are not always financial in nature, nor do they always take place in your office. A spring BBQ or lecture by a gardening specialist work just as well in fostering membership in your community of clients.
3. They are advertised well in advance with attractive marketing materials.
4. Attendees are strongly encouraged to bring guests and are reminded of this more than once.
5. At the event, there is a procedure in place to capture information from guests who attend so that they can request an appointment if they wish to meet with you.

Not every client will refer, but for those who do, you need to address questions they may have, whether they are articulated or not. For example, the referral process must outline the experience the person being referred will have. By informing your client of this, and by then delivering upon it, you mitigate any concerns your client and the person they refer may have, thereby reinforcing the referral-generating behavior.

Alternatively, they may be concerned you're going to start 'selling' the person they refer as soon as you get them in the door. You need to let your client know that your first objective is to determine if you and their referral are right for each other, that it would be inappropriate to sell anything to a prospect. Your goal is to evaluate alignment, to do nothing that would reflect poorly on the client and to do everything that reflects how highly you think of the client for having made the referral in the first place.

Let's continue with our Reboot Meeting and consider how to weave in an effective referral message. I've made assumptions concerning the Ideal Client that the advisor will refer to in the following example:

Script: *"It's hard to believe we've already been working together this long. How would you say your experience with our firm has been so far?" [Client responds.]*

"Before we start our Financial Review, there is something important I want to speak about with you. I mentioned that you are exactly the type of client I value working with, and it is a delight knowing you. You are typical of the clients I work with: You're a [professional/business owner, within 7-10 years of retirement and maintaining a fun, active retirement lifestyle]. You have investible assets of [$XXX], and I am your exclusive financial advisor. You fully participate in our meetings and in our client events. You ask questions and are willing to implement the strategies we discuss. You show that you appreciate the high level of service I try to consistently deliver."

Message: I've let you know again how important you are to me, and I've shared with you the reasons why you are an Ideal Client of mine.

Script: *"You may recall when we first met today that I told you it was never my goal to be all things to everyone, but rather all things to a few. Not everyone would want a Personal CFO, and frankly not everyone needs one. For that reason, I keep my practice fairly small.*

"However, from time to time, openings do come up. And in my experience, the best way to fill those openings is with the friends and family members of my best clients – clients just like you. So here's the offer I would like to extend. In my schedule each week, I leave one or two appointments open for referrals from my top clients. So if you ever know of anyone who you think could use my help, just give me a call and we can discuss it. I don't claim to be a miracle worker, but I'll always do my very best to help them."

Message: Just in case I didn't have to tell you about needing all of your assets under my care and therefore describe the new configuration of my practice, let me tell you now. And one more time, feel the love – I can't tell you often enough how much I value you. If you know of someone who I can help, let me know.

Script: *"I will then call them and send them the same Introduction Package I sent to you for this meeting. I will schedule with them what I call an Alignment Meeting to determine if we should work together. I will keep you in the loop right up until they become a client – or up to the point where a decision is made regarding whether we'll work together.*

"Regardless of whether we agree to work together or not, I will promise you that I will treat anyone you send here with the utmost respect and professionalism. Even if they don't become a client, they will appreciate the meeting, and your recommendation of me will reflect well on you.

"Keep this in mind as well: sometimes people don't feel comfortable making an appointment with an advisor they've never met. So if it's easier, you can bring them to any of my events."

Message: Here's what they can expect, and here's what you can expect. I am open to your referrals in any manner you may request. You never have to fear looking bad in the eyes of a friend or family member. I will provide value to you and your referral no matter the outcome.

You've now completed the Reboot portion of your meeting and are able to start the Financial Review as laid out in your agenda. At this point, I am presuming that you've been a financial advisor long enough to know how this works. Just be sure that any new information you uncover gets recorded after the meeting in the client's CLAN information. Some of these changes will offer you opportunities to begin further work (for example, estate planning, asset transfers) or make referrals to members of your financial advisory network of related professionals (for example, to a lawyer for Powers of Attorney, Wills).

Following the Reboot Meeting, you want to make sure that all the messages and goodwill you imparted to your client are not quickly forgotten. Send your client a handwritten card of acknowledgment, preferably one that is not firm branded but one that is unique and original. It needs to be personal and authentic in sentiment. It doesn't have to say anything more than that you enjoyed seeing them and that you appreciate the trust and confidence they have placed in you. Then let them know to be in touch if there is any further service you can provide. Signed, You.

PROCESS FOUR: NEW CLIENT ONBOARDING

The New Client Onboarding process affords you the opportunity to frame a prospective client's perception from their very first encounter with your revitalized, experience-centric practice. Always remember: any client relationship is a direct result of how it began.

While client onboarding is the last process in this chapter, in many ways it is most important because it establishes for all clients going forward the foundation of their experience and relationship with your practice. Through it, you ensure that you achieve the greatest possible alignment with a prospective client because clients who are most closely aligned with their advisor are the most predisposed to providing referrals.

What may be fundamentally different about this process – and somewhat of a challenge for many advisors to get their heads around – is that you may not end up taking this prospect on. How you handle this situation – which arose from a referral from one of your best clients – will reflect your integrity as a professional to the client who referred, to the prospect, to your firm, to your team and to yourself. It's a tall order. No one likes to 'not make the cut' – and yet that possibility exists. Therefore, what you say and how you say it is critical.

If you engage in any type of sales process, even one that is 'consultative,' you are still manipulating to 'close' the prospect. Remember, your purpose is to make a lasting impression that will differentiate you from every other advisor your prospect has ever had or met. Wouldn't you prefer to reach a common understanding of what it is you offer, what makes you unique? Wouldn't you rather manage their entire portfolio, and have them refer other like-minded investors who would also value your unique and specific approach?

Here's the situation: you've received a referral from one of your best clients. You've called that client and obtained a little background information on the person they've referred. You – not your assistant – contact the referral directly and schedule to meet. You send the client who made the referral a handwritten thank-you card. Whether or not their friend or family member becomes one of your clients doesn't have any bearing on the gratitude you show when a valued client refers.

Now your assistant can jump in, mailing out an Introduction package similar to the one mailed ahead of the Reboot Meeting, with the following additions and omissions:

- An agenda that itemizes the following topics: Meeting Overview, About Our Company/ Clients/Services, Our Process, Goals and Objectives, How We Will Proceed, Next Step.
- Third-party articles that bolster your position on investing or that profile you.
- Printed directions to your office and parking instructions.
- A cover letter that clearly states the prospect does not have to bring any financial information to the meeting. The meeting is solely an opportunity for both parties (you and the prospect) to get to know each other, and for the prospect to learn about your approach so that he or she may determine whether or not they wish to show you their personal financial information.
- No information on products or specific services your firm might offer. When you send someone a prospectus or a product overview, what you are saying is "eventually I am going to ask you to buy this."

Welcoming your prospective client is no different than welcoming your best client to a review meeting. They are met in the lobby, escorted to the meeting room, offered refreshments, and the meeting starts on time. Why go to the trouble and expense over someone you may never do further business with? Because the caliber of your referrals from your best clients warrants it. Because the reflection back onto your best client warrants it. Because the reflection onto your code of conduct and experience process warrants it. Because the entirety of your team's efforts and your firm's reputation warrant it. Should this prospect become a client who hands to you their entire portfolio and refers clients, the cost will be recovered and then some.

The Alignment Meeting

At the outset of this chapter, we covered the purpose of right-sizing your practice so that the clients you were left with were ones you chose and who chose you right back. The New Client Onboarding process mirrors the necessity for this approach. It incorporates several meetings so that you have the opportunity to professionally assess whether this client meets the attributes of your Ideal Client profile without placing pressure on either of you to commit after one meeting. We therefore call this first meeting The Alignment Meeting.

After you sit down with your prospective client, you need to make the following important points:

- You appreciate that they have taken time to meet you.
- This meeting is about sharing information, to help you both determine whether or not there is merit to exploring a long-term relationship.
- You are selective about whom you take on as a client, and you expect that they are also going to be very careful in choosing an advisor.
- At the end of this meeting, you will both pick a suitable date for a follow-up (typically 3 days), and that before such time, neither you nor the prospective client will be asked to make a decision about working together.

This approach is intended to put the prospective client at ease so that they may be relaxed, confident, and open to sharing information.

Determining alignment means uncovering information about attitudes and expectations, listening carefully and sizing up. As a process, Client Onboarding is like the Reboot Meeting, with its own scripting and messaging. To start the meeting, ask the prospect to describe what they feel a financial advisor does for a client. Then ask them to describe their expectations if you both agree to work together. Believe it or not, studies show that this is the first thing clients want to know about an advisor. They don't want to know how you are paid – not yet. They don't want to know about your firm – not yet. They want to know how you will take care of them. Are you easy to understand? How will you manage them? Through this information, they will arrive at an assumption about your ethic as an advisor.

Most potential clients will tell you that they appreciate meetings and telephone calls, and that they feel better knowing that any potential problems will be cleared up quickly. As for returns, typically you will be told a story – they will tell you what they have to invest, the value of their house, and how they would like to live in retirement.

Script: *"Before we go any further, I'd like to return to your definition of what it is I do. You said that I build retirement and financial plans using various investments such as mutual funds, annuities and life insurance – that is exactly what I do.*

"However, you will recall that at the beginning of this meeting I said that I do some things a little differently. I'd like to be clear about this, specifically about my approach. Many financial advisors strive to grow a large practice. I do not do that. I would prefer to keep a smaller number of clients who appreciate this level of service and commitment.

"My clients consider me their Personal CFO. I typically manage a family's entire portfolio, and I help them navigate all of their critical financial planning decisions."

With this message, you show that you listen carefully, that you have terms of engagement, and you state what those terms are.

Your next objective is to determine if assets are held elsewhere.

Script: *"I'd like to comment on your expectations for service and returns. Clearly, today isn't the day that we are going to discuss your portfolio. But I do want to touch on what you said because I want you to know that I heard you.*

"You indicated that you have $XXX to invest, that you have approximately $XXX equity in your home and that you hope to retire in the next 5 to 7 years. Furthermore, funding education for your children/grandchildren is important, and you would like to lead an active lifestyle in retirement.

"The $XXX in investments that you discussed – is this all of your investments, or does this amount refer to the investments that you are considering investing with me?"

If this prospective client indicates that there are additional investments that they were not considering placing with you, ignore it for now. You will return to this point. For now, you will introduce the concept of process, which expands upon your explanation of the services you provide clients:

Script: *"Your financial goals sound reasonable, given your age, investible assets etc.*

"I have a process that I follow with each of my clients. If we agree to work together, we will follow this process very carefully. I will explain that process in a few minutes.

"I would like to comment on what you said was important to you from a service perspective. You said meetings, telephone calls as well as a frustration with small nagging service issues. I appreciated what you had to say. It tells me that you value contact and communication. Most of my clients feel the same way. So I would like to tell you how I

structure my service to keep everyone happy and confident that I have everything in control.

"I meet with my clients at least [x] times each year, and unlike a lot of other advisors, I ensure that my meetings are booked well in advance so that you always know exactly when we will meet, and you will always be sent an agenda. If either of us needs to reschedule, we'll let each other know well in advance. I call each of my clients every 90 days without fail, just to check in. If we miss each other, and you have nothing to report on your end, you don't have to return my call if you are too busy. However, if I ever leave you a message asking you to call me back, then I need you to do that, because something has come up that needs your input."

This all seems pretty simple and straightforward, right? What it's saying, however, is that your process has clarity and serves to meet expectations.

Spend a little time asking the prospect what they know about your firm. This isn't so much about what they know as it is about you wanting them to understand your choice for being there. Your firm is the environment in which you choose to offer your professional services. Knowing what criteria were important to you in choosing this firm will tell your prospects a lot about what kind of person you are.

Describe the firm's commitment to your personal and professional growth, providing examples, and your appreciation of that commitment. If appropriate, describe the support you receive from your general manager, the excellence of your back office, and provide examples *("they process orders, requests and any other administrative queries quickly, clearly and consistently")* and why this is important to you. Avoid any temptation to discuss specific products, proprietary investments or services. The moment you say "and we have excellent products," you become a salesperson. And your prospect can find a salesperson anywhere.

Your next objective introduces your Ideal Client Profile.

Script: *"Now that you are aware of why I am here at [ABC], I would like you to understand the profile of my typical client."*

At this point, you would describe your Ideal Client as was illustrated previously in the Reboot Meeting script. To this description, you would add:

Script: *"My clients value my process, and they participate in it. They attend my meetings, ask questions and generally inspect what they expect. Over my career, I have seen time and again that it's better for both parties if we meet regularly and keep these appointments.*

"Throughout the year, I host a number of client events and seminars. My clients try to make as many as possible. Again, I work hard to ensure I am bringing the best topics possible. My clients appreciate that and want to hear what I have to say."

From a general overview of your client process, you now narrow to the specific onboarding process so that the prospect will know what to expect.

Script: *"At various times today, I have mentioned my process, which is pretty straight forward. I'd like to show you exactly what that process is so that you are clear about how our relationship would be structured."*

Present the prospect with a copy of the Reboot Meeting agenda, which mirrors a Review Meeting agenda except for the exclusion of the fourth item, the review of your firm, compensation and process, which you are already covering in this meeting. This will allow your prospect to gain a clear understanding of what will be covered whenever they meet with you.

Script: *"Should we agree to work together, we would meet again in approximately two weeks. This would be our first official financial meeting, and you would be required to bring in all of your paperwork and documents. We will use this first meeting to see where we are at, and what, if any, adjustments need to be made to your plan. I will provide you with a checklist of items that I will require you to bring to the meeting, and my assistant is available to help you if you have any questions. Once we have your portfolio set up and on track, we will meet at least[x] times each year – and we will follow similar agendas."*

Some advisors actually host three review meetings each year in addition to all of their other client offerings, using two for portfolio reviews and one "just to talk," often off-site. Clients come to know that this third meeting is just as important to you as the other two. Furthermore, many advisors find that this third meeting, which is typically more relaxed, is an excellent opportunity to reinforce the relationship or uncover new opportunities.

Before the meeting ends, you need to address the issue of your compensation. Voluntarily disclosing this information is often a significant point of differentiation from other advisors.

Script: *"Now that we have gone through my approach, my typical client, and how I work with my clients, you are probably wondering how I get paid. I charge a fee of [$X] on your investments. My fee covers [list everything covered]. Should you require any additional work done, there will be a charge of [$XXX/hr]. Rarely, if ever, would you require anything outside of the usual services, but I like to be as clear and transparent as possible."*

The Alignment Meeting is essentially now over. After asking the prospect if there are any further questions, tell them:

Script: *"I want to thank you for coming to meet me today. I enjoyed meeting you, and I hope you feel as good about our meeting as I do. As I said when we first sat down, I am not going to ask you to make a decision today.*

"I am going to discuss everything I learned today with my team. I'd like you to consider what you learned today as well. Take a few days to consider everything I told you and whether or not you feel you could be happy here. If we both feel that we have a fit, then we will begin the process by booking an appointment and getting started."

Arrange to call them in three days with the outcome of your assessment as to whether they are suitable for bringing on board. By allowing the Prospect the privacy and time to make an important decision about working together, you've broken the pattern of manipulation that is inherent in the sales process. The moment your prospective client leaves, send a hand-written note, thanking them for their time and letting them know you enjoyed meeting them.

Three days later, call them. If the prospective client tells you up front that they have not made a decision yet or express that they need more time to decide, they are politely telling you "no." If you had wanted to bring them on board, you might say:

Script: *"I understand that it may not be the right time for you right now. I enjoyed meeting you and would welcome the opportunity to explore this relationship further in the future.*

"When you are in a position to make a decision or have more time, give me a call. The door will always be open and we can revisit things then. From time to time, we are in touch with people. Would it be all right if I were to contact you?"

If the prospect is more definite in their reply about not wishing to work with you, let them know you enjoyed meeting them and ask if you might contact them in the future. If they agree, schedule a follow-up call for six months out.

If, instead, you have decided that the prospect does not meet your client criteria:

Script: *"It was a pleasure meeting you the other day. I have considered everything we talked about, and I believe that I am not well aligned with you and the outcomes you desire. I got a sense that you were looking for [provide a reason, for example, returns that you cannot provide, a discount on fees, unrealistic about your expectations for service, etc.] As a result, I would recommend that you seek out an advisor who specializes in [outcome]. I would be happy to recommend another advisor who may be a match for you."*

If both of you agree in moving forward together, arrange to meet with them to review their portfolio.

Many advisors consider agreement after the Alignment Meeting as verification that the client is coming on board. However, without having seen their asset holdings, other advisors choose to insert a proviso that only after this information is disclosed can they give approval to the onboarding process. My feeling is that your comfort level determines when you wish to make clear to the prospect that they are becoming a client – before their portfolio review or after. Because you have minimum assets-under-care criteria, you may wish to approve afterwards. Chances are that you have already picked up clues about their holdings based on their description of goals during the Alignment Meeting, the relationship they have with the client who referred them, and so on. Regardless of whether you insert a financial review proviso, your approach and scripting would be the same.

Once you have completed your review of their portfolio and met to determine solutions (The Solutions Meeting), you will introduce to your new client your referral process, exactly as you have during your Reboot Meetings with existing clients. You will position it as a service you are able to provide for their friends and family members, and that there is no obligation on the new client's part – or an expectation on yours – that they ever provide referrals. And that is the truth. For while your strategy is to grow your business through referrals, you over-riding intent is to take care of this new client. Only through that care will they become your advocate.

Only a few more steps now remain in the New Client Onboarding Process:

1. The day after the Solutions Meeting, send your new client a thank-you card, again one that is not firm-branded but instead of stylish design and written in your own hand, welcoming the new client on board.
2. Two weeks after the Solutions Meeting, your assistant sends a Welcome letter that informs the new client of all team members, what they do, their contact information and your firm's hours of operation. This differs from the corporate brochure that was included in your Introduction package because it is personally written.
3. Four weeks after the Solutions Meeting, your assistant places a Care Call, just to see if there are questions about the information they may have received from your office, such as transfer forms, new statements. This step focuses communication with your office to your staff while reinforcing the message that you are being mindful of their best interests.

ONE OTHER PROCESS: THE MOMENT OF TRUTH

Okay, so I fibbed in this chapter's title. There is one more process in the menu of experiences you have now decided to deliver, one we call The Moment of Truth. That's just a term for acknowledging major milestones in your clients' lives.

And becoming a client of yours is a major life event. You didn't think it was, be honest. That's perhaps because you are still holding onto a few old ideas about what you do. In your new and reinvigorated practice, however, your importance and worth to your new client – to all yours clients – cannot be undervalued. Their lives going forward will be forever changed by having you, their new personal CFO, managing their financial affairs.

They are now members of an exclusive community under your care. This moment needs to be recognized.

You're not in the business of buying a client's loyalty or goodwill, so I ask that you keep that in mind as you read the following. A Moment of Truth is fundamentally different than giving gifts. It is recognition of achievement, just like retirement, a new home, a new child or a new son-in-law.

Five days after your new client has completed their first financial solutions meeting – or five days after your Reboot Meeting – send a moment of truth gift with a note of appreciation. It can be an ornament, a small piece of art, a framed print, a coin collector book with a current year silver dollar inside (in fact, this last item lends itself nicely to an annual Moment of Truth gift that follows a Reboot Meeting). Whatever you send, it should be tasteful and it must have quality. It doesn't have to be a Montblanc pen, but neither should it be a foreign-made knock off with your corporate name on it.

Regardless of what it is, it will arrive completely unexpectedly, and will instantly reinforce to your client that they are working with the right advisor.

POSITIONING YOUR INTENT

In looking back over the script samples of the Reboot Meeting, the importance of positioning your v*alue proposition* and a*lignment statement* has been a constant consideration. The goal here is twofold. First, you want your clients never to forget why they started working with you. Secondly, you want to remind them of the ongoing benefits they receive from being your client. Achieving these two goals will keep you referable.

Establish Personal Meaning

Consumer behaviors are generally predictable. Your clients talk to others about products or services that they have pleasantly experienced. The more they talk about something they enjoyed, the more they trust it themselves.

It follows that when you are top of mind, your clients are more likely to share whatever key messaging you have imparted when they discuss you with a friend or family member.

So ask yourself: are the key messages you have been reiterating to your clients personal, specific and easily communicated to another person? Not only during the Reboot Meeting and New Client Onboarding Process, but in all of your communications? How much jargon do you use, and is it making the right impression on a client? Do you talk in abstract concepts that clients may not fully understand?

When communicating key messages to clients, position your service in the most personal way you can. Describe how your service fills a need. Here are some examples:

Figure 3: Samples of Impersonal Language vs. Personal Meaning

Impersonal/Abstract/Jargon	Personal
We use asset allocation to mitigate risk and ensure that our clients take on an appropriate amount of volatility for their comfort zone.	*Investing is not a short-term event. We are your partners in a process of balanced long-term investment management through thick and thin.*
You need growth in your portfolio to offset the long-term effects of inflation.	*We work with you to try and keep ahead of the increased costs of living.*
We provide you with a detailed financial plan that assesses your risks and gives you action items to offset those risks and achieve your goals.	*We provide a financial blueprint so that you can sleep at night.*
We build trusting relationships with our clients and ensure that our investment and financial strategy recommendations are aligned with a client's goals.	*Our clients sleep well at night.*

Another method of establishing personal meaning is to adopt a general-to-specific manner of explaining concepts to your clients. This method is effective for describing the value of what you do by illustrating personal benefits instead of conveying abstractions that may be unclear. Some examples are:

Figure 4: Samples of General-to-Specific Concept Explanations

You Say	You Refine	You Elaborate
"We use tactical asset allocation to manage client portfolios."	*"This approach allows us to take advantage of the changing value of certain asset classes."*	*"For instance, no matter what is happening in the economy or the market, we are positioned for opportunity."*
"We are cash flow based financial planners."	*"Focusing on cash flow is more meaningful than focusing on the financial markets."*	*"For instance, peace of mind about your cash flow allows you to not focus on short term fluctuations in the market."*
"Our desire is to be your Personal CFO."	*"You will be required to make important decisions about your financial future."*	*"For instance, we will be a source of trusted advice that you can rely on when making important decisions."*

Without personal meaning, you run the risk of overloading your client with abstract concepts or jargon that have little to do with what you actually provide. Making it personal allows a client to internalize and create his own opinion about the value you bring to the table.

Team Alignment: Leverage the Group

Teams which are highly referable have a common and understood expectation that everything they do as individuals and as a team is focused on generating referrals from satisfied clients.

Everyone on your team, including part-time or temporary help, must have a consistent and aligned perception of the end value of each activity they complete.

An excellent case study for observing the powerful result of a highly successful, collective team effort is to revisit the 60,000 cast members employed by Disney World in Orlando, Florida. The Magic Kingdom welcomed their 17 millionth guest in 2011. Each guest's experience is the primary focus of every cast member every day that they report to work. This is because Disney strives to create a positive, repeatable, consistent experience for every person who walks through the entrance gates, no matter if they are the 17 millionth guest or not. It is through deliberate efforts to align employees with the client experience that a huge operation like Disney World can create a consistent, high-level experience that makes visiting them so referable.

It goes without saying that if Disney World can create alignment across 60,000 employees, then a financial advisor can do the same across his or her team. The secret is in being obsessed with the end result – creating an experience that a client will want to refer others to.

Trust reflects the goodwill you have with your clients, and in a service business, goodwill is paramount. It is a predictor of the level of loyalty that clients will have and correlates directly to the amount of return business that the company enjoys. Goodwill is typically the driving factor that turns a customer into a client, and a client into an advocate who, in turn, provides referrals.

Trust is made up of four attributes, all of which MUST be authentic.

1. **Accountability.** There is nothing that erodes a client relationship faster than not being accountable. Being accountable demonstrates an obligation and willingness to accept responsibility for individual or team actions. Willingness to be responsible and not deflect issues or situations earns every member of the team respect and trust.
2. **Integrity.** Integrity is the reflection of individual and team character, conveying an adherence to moral and ethical principles. This soundness of character is what invites – and is attractive to – higher levels of client trust.
3. **Chemistry.** Relationships are all about connecting with another person, of finding what is popularly called 'chemistry'. This intan-

gible element is something to which all great relationship managers constantly pay attention. Chemistry can only ramp higher with clients who implicitly trust you.

4. **Credibility.** If you and your team are prepared to deliver your experience processes flawlessly, your actions will inspire belief in the quality of your enterprise. When you or your team fail to meet an expectation, the perception of quality is eroded.

RECAP

Four key processes – right-sizing your practice, educating current clients about your rebranded practice, positioning for referral-generation, and onboarding new clients – will form the foundation of converting the services you currently provide clients and prospects into experiences. A fifth process, the Moment of Truth, is an adjunct process to the Reboot and New Client Onboarding experiences.

Right-sizing your practice frees you and your team of wasted time and energy so that you may devote more attention to your remaining clients, all of whom fit your Ideal Client Profile. Sometimes sorry has to be the hardest word.

Existing clients need to be informed of your new order of business. This is achieved through the Reboot Meeting, the first review meeting you will have which each client. In the Reboot Meeting, you review your process of taking care of them, how you are able to function as their personal CFO, why all their assets need to be moved to your car, how you can help anyone they choose to refer to you, and you demonstrate your integrity and professionalism as an advisor with whom they choose to do all their business.

Enhancing client-driven referrals is your primary business-building method. As such, you need to show your clients that you are highly referable, and you need to let them know what will happen should they refer someone to you.

Onboarding new clients is a multi-step process that allows both you and a prospect the opportunity to assess whether you are a beneficial fit for each other. You are able to determine if they meet your criteria for being an Ideal Client. Several meetings are held, the first of which is the Alignment Meeting where you get to know each other and where you explain your process. If you both agree to work together, a second meeting is arranged for you to conduct a financial review of their portfolio. You may or may not wish to make this meeting a second phase of alignment, determining whether their existing holdings also meet your criteria for an Ideal Client. The Solutions Meeting, if not part of the financial review meeting, converts the prospect into a client.

Moments of Truth are opportunities for you to recognize a client's achievement of a major milestone. Coming aboard as a client is one such event.

Your ability to persuade and educate your clients is enhanced by imparting value using language they will understand. Your team is an extension of you, and all of your team abides by this same approach. The result is that your clients trust you because you provide accountability, integrity, personal chemistry with them and credibility.

Chapter 8

Centers of Influence and Your FAN Club

YOU WANT TO BRING AS much value to your clients as you possibly can, and an exceptional way of doing that is through a financial advice network (FAN).

Creating a FAN is not an easy task. It involves as much time and energy to implement as the process you created to build your base of affluent clients. You may ask yourself, "Is this degree of effort going to be worth it? I have spent considerable time and effort building my client base. Why bother with a FAN when I can simply enjoy the benefits of my client referrals?"

It is actually *your responsibility* to recommend professionals who do excellent work.

Unless you are completely confident that you are indispensable and irreplaceable to each and every affluent client under your care, you need to secure the relationship you have with them. Being the hub of a trusted, competent FAN will help you build a virtual wall around your client. The value of your relationships with your clients will increase exponentially as you secure your role of being their Personal CFO by leveraging your FAN.

Providing your clients with a directory of professionals whom you recommend is an excellent value-add.

There are three important FANs that directly affect the growth of your practice and the value you bring others:

1. Your FAN of like-minded professionals (Centers of Influence, or COIs) to whom you can refer your clients and prospects.
2. The FANs of your strategically-aligned COIs, of which you are a member.
3. Your clients' FANS, all of those professionals who influence the financial decisions your clients make.

Your goal is to become the axis of all of these FANs, to bring them together under the umbrella of the experience you provide.

Your financial advice network represents a lot of value to your clients, which adds to your own perceived value. A FAN plays on the idea that through exceptional service, experience and partnership, you can create happy FANs of both you and your practice.

What you have to be most concerned with is choosing the right candidates to be in your network. You are looking for entrepreneurially-minded professionals who are as committed to their own practices as you are when it comes to delivering an exceptional experience.

I want to encourage you to think outside of the usual suspects of lawyers and accountants, and to include a broad network of professionals – real estate agents, renovation contractors, estate settlement services, home-staging experts, caterers and the like – whom you trust and respect and to whom you would, without hesitation, refer an existing client.

Imagine you are meeting with either a prospective client or an existing one, and they tell you that they are going to sell their business or that they are considering the purchase of a franchise. How impressive would it be if you were able to quarterback an introduction to an accountant or a lawyer who can help with the process?

Take it a step further. Imagine you not only quarterbacked the meeting, but you hosted it and managed all communication, briefing your client so that he felt well-represented, well-prepared and simply needed to show up for the meeting.

Imagine all these professionals at your office, and you have seized this opportunity to shine. Lunch is catered, your client feels cared for, your professional FAN partners look good. Your client accepts their offer of business, and your partners have had the opportunity to see you in action.

How many meetings like that would it take for one of these professionals to feel comfortable enough to refer someone to you?

Your desire to help – to expend the energy and time to coordinate this meeting – transforms the experience and enhances the relationship you have with your client and the relationships you have with your aligned partners. This is your commitment to be a Personal CFO in action, just as you promised to your clients.

Ultimately, you only want to work with professionals whom you can trust. That's it. And you want to make a point of having all of your clients work with your partners because then you can operate with more certainty about the influences affecting your clients' financial decisions.

At the outset, you have to be prepared for resistance from your potential partnering FAN. It is doubtful that lawyers or accountants will be as motivated – and as up to speed – on the necessity of an exceptional client experience as you are. Therefore, be prepared that you may have to lead by example. You will have to be the primary mover on this one. Be patient and wait for it to catch on. The more value you add to your partners, the more irreplaceable you become to them.

I met an advisor in Florida named Greg who works for a major bank. When we first met, he didn't have very many assets under management, but his commitment to being an exceptional Personal CFO was evident.

Greg set about building his business through building his FAN. He took the time to put together an introduction kit on his practice and his process, and he set up several meetings with accountants in his area.

As you know, one good partner who has a high opinion of you can change your business overnight.

Greg didn't go out looking for referrals. He set out looking for the right accountants who he could trust sending his clients to. Trust in their work ethic and ability to deliver meant everything to Greg. He needed to know that whoever was associated with him was as committed to delivering an incredible experience as he was.

He found one or two people who fit the bill. They were so impressed with Greg and to his commitment to help his clients that when the opportunities presented themselves, they sent some of their clients Greg's way.

I don't have to tell you how this trickles down. Greg now manages ten times the assets he did when I met him only a few years ago.

The process of developing a FAN takes time. To build trusted mutually beneficial associations, you need to prove your credibility to other professionals, and this means making frequent and meaningful contact with them. Start by building your FAN team from professionals already working with your preferred clients.

It is important to select your referral partners carefully because when you recommend someone, your clients trust your opinion. A positive experience will stay in a person's mind and encourage them to return to you for additional advice. On the other hand, it only takes one bad experience to sour a relationship. Be informed and confident about the quality of work your referral partner can provide.

It might be easy to remember that Mr. Smith is a CPA or Ms. Taylor is an estate lawyer. But what makes them stand out? Take time to sit down with other professionals and learn about their unique selling propositions. By spending this time to learn about their specialties, you will be able to provide a more qualified referral. And reciprocate; use this opportunity to identify how you work with clients and why your services are worth recommending.

The goal is to learn everything you can about your selected professional's business, the services he or she offers and more about them as individuals and owners. In return, allow them to do the same thing with you and your business. If you both feel that you can work well together, you will have the information needed to intelligently refer business to each other. In addition, your clients will benefit from having access to your network. They will perceive you as a well-connected expert in your field who goes above and beyond what is expected of most financial advisors.

FAN: THE PRE-EMPTIVE STRIKE

Think of your best clients. Who coordinates their financial plans? You know that the answer should be, *I do!* However, unless you know who their other professional advisors are, you cannot answer this question with any degree of certainty. One of the greatest threats to a financial advisor occurs when a client gives another advisor the opportunity to look at his financial plan.

It would be easy to say that clients allow this situation to happen because they don't have a relationship with their advisor based on an inherent level of trust. In truth, however, it's the opposite. Advisors allow this to happen because they haven't made the effort to build trusting relationships with their clients.

Affluent people talk to other affluent people. Introductions to other advisors are the result of a personal recommendation made by a family member or friend. Or a professional such as an accountant may recommend an advisor to his client. Clients are open to this type of professional recommendation because they already trust the professional who is making the recommendation.

If you attend to your role as Personal CFO, this type of incident is less likely to occur because you become the link between your clients and the financial professionals involved in implementing their financial plan.

I refer to this specialized team of other professional advisors as your client's FAN. It is not at all surprising that the affluent client you may be onboarding would already arrive into your practice supported by an existing network of outside professionals. This situation can lead to the financial affairs of this affluent client unfolding both predictably and randomly, subject to the influences beyond your control or knowledge. It therefore becomes imperative that you discover who these other advisors so that you may better position yourself as your client's CFO.

There are three key benefits to building your Financial Advice Network:

1. Your client will benefit from your solid, reliable and trustworthy FAN. They will recommend you to other affluent people who seek this type of comprehensive service.

2. Professionals you recommend are more likely to remain loyal to you as a source for business. This reduces the risk that they will recommend other advisors to your clients.
3. You secure your position as the primary relationship in your clients' FAN.

You need to keep in mind some basic and important facts about affluent clients and how their FANs operate.

First, affluent clients rely on more than one professional for their financial affairs, people like accountants, trust managers, insurance providers and so on. Typically, a financial advisor will deal with investment advice but will defer to other professionals for tax preparation, estate planning, banking and insurance. Do you know who the professionals are who work with your clients? That's why positioning yourself as a CFO who quarterbacks your client's influencers is so important. If you cannot be the one who recommends these professionals to your clients, at the very least you should be the one coordinating their services.

Keep in mind, too, that just because your client has these professionals within their existing FAN, it does not necessarily follow that your client is satisfied with the services provided by these professionals. Ask the important questions, and be prepared with a recommendation if the answer is in the negative.

Secondly, in the majority of cases, a client is recommended to a FAN contact by a friend, family member, associate or by another professional in the client's FAN. In fact, studies show that 77% of high net worth individuals will only choose an advisor based on a referral from someone they know. Your goal is become the person directing these recommendations. The client-advisor relationship should be the primary relationship within your client's FAN.

Thirdly, a client's FAN members usually work in isolation. As a result, proactive advisors have the opportunity to take the leading role in the FAN by integrating the members of the group so that everyone is working together towards the same client goals and objectives.

Each member of the FAN has a unique ability that can add strength to the overall client experience. Like advisors, other FAN members encourage and welcome recommendations and introductions to prospective clients.

BUILDING YOUR FAN: A PROCESS

There are several ways to go about developing a group of professionals for FAN. Start with your best clients. Ask each of them who the members of their Financial Advice Network are. Be specific. Learn who their lawyers, accountants, bankers, insurance agents and estate planners are. Every name represents a potential professional relationship you may wish to develop. Find out from your clients what they think of them.

Discover, as well, the professionals with whom your clients are disappointed. Your clients' dissatisfaction is a golden opportunity for you to recommend a member of your FAN. Everyone benefits when you are able to recommend a good replacement. Your client is happy to have someone who satisfies, your position as FAN director is consolidated, and you have another opportunity to build on the trust you have established with your client.

Contact each identified professional and arrange an introductory meeting. Explain that you would like to talk about the client you have in common. Remember, these are your *best* clients' FAN members. At the very least, meeting with them is smart business sense.

The first meeting you will have with a potential FAN member is all about alignment and gathering CLAN information that can be used to further your relationship in the future.

When you meet, and once pleasantries are out of the way, move the conversation to the purpose of the meeting. Inform them that you were recommended by one of your best clients, and that you are interested in learning more about what they do. You want to understand why your best client recommended this person. Indicate that, from time to time, you have the opportunity to recommend to clients quality services that compliment the services you provide.

Script: *"Given sufficient knowledge about each of our services, I feel we may complement each other. You have been highly referred by [client], and I am always looking to establish relationships with professionals in other fields who are known for their superb customer service and business ethics."*

Educate them about your process: who you are, what you do and how you do it. Let them know about your Alignment Meeting process with a prospective client so that they have an example of how you would handle a new client they were to send your way.

In turn, ask them to provide you with a business overview and to describe what they feel makes them unique. You'll want to get a sense of the following:

1. How long they've been in business.
2. Their unique selling proposition.
3. What differentiates them from their competition.
4. What practices they adhere to that ensure their clients remain happy.
5. Any new marketing strategies and the results they hope to achieve over the next 12 to 24 months.
6. The procedure that a new client goes through.
7. Their primary goals.
8. What they look for in a strategic partner.
9. What they consider to be the most important qualities in a financial professional.
10. Personal interests, and how they seem to be balancing work with personal pursuits. Alignment with members of your FAN is just as important as it is with your clients.

Many financial advisors make the mistake of expecting reciprocation with accountants and attorneys when they simply refer a client's business to them. Have you ever experienced giving multiple referrals to an accountant or lawyer only to be left forgotten at their subsequent client meetings?

This happens because giving someone business is not a sufficient enough incentive for people to do the same.

You need to make *recommendations.* This is very different than giving a referral. When you make a recommendation, it assumes a transfer of trust from one professional to another. Most professionals will not risk losing a client's trust by making light of a recommendation made to another professional. For this reason, you must develop a high degree of trust with your Financial Advice Network members.

How might you differentiate yourself to a member of your FAN in order to foster that trust? How do you move from giving referrals to making recommendations? You must construct and consistently deliver a deliberate, meaningful service process for your FAN members and potential FAN members, one that demonstrates consistency, integrity and accountability. The rule of relationship building is to be patient, as it will take time, and to have frequent, genuine contact.

In this way, a FAN member is much like a client. Create an experience process for the professionals who interact with your office on a regular basis. Incorporate into your FAN process quarterly phone calls, articles of interest, invitations to select client events, copies of your newsletter and annual anchors (such as Thanksgiving/birthday cards). Once you have decided on your approach, enter it into your contact management system to ensure that you consistently follow through on it. As recommendations start to come back to you, send an acknowledgment for the *trust and confidence,* not for the business. You want to recognize their trust over and above everything else.

RECAP

Developing a Financial Advisory Network (FAN) of like-minded professionals to whom you may recommend your clients and who will reciprocate by recommending you to their clients is one of your most effective ways of building your business. In addition, it insulates your clients from being poached by other advisors and reinforces your role as their Personal CFO.

Finding professionals to become members of your FAN begins by asking your best clients who they are working with. These queries will also uncover opportunities for you to recommend professionals in place of those with whom they are not satisfied.

Bringing FAN members on board and caring for the relationship requires processes similar to those provided to your clients. You first need to determine if you are aligned as business owners and professionals. Then you need to ensure that you show your appreciation for the trust and confidence they have shown by recommending their clients to you.

Chapter 9

Are You Experienced?

YOU'VE MADE IT THROUGH the meat and potatoes of this book. Along the way, I hope you've become inspired to look at your practice and your life a little differently. That was, after all, my intention.

I've talked a lot about processes and how they can be shaped to deliver exceptional experiences to your clients. I feel I've made a case for the vitality and urgency of the Experience model. It's not the only option out there, as I've shown. But it is the only one that should matter to you. It is the only one that will transform you and your business. It has become a huge differentiator, and it is here to stay.

So to serve as a summary and a coda, let's look at the Experience Economy from an evolutionary and global perspective one final time.

WHAT IS THE EXPERIENCE ECONOMY?

The Experience Economy is the latest level in the evolution of commercial exchange which began when humans began bartering one thing in exchange for another. Commodities are generally regarded as the first, the rawest and the dominant unit of exchange going back into pre-recorded history. An example would be gold or a goat.

With time, the dominance of commodities was overtaken by the trade of goods or products, which were essentially commodities with value added. An example of this evolution would be raw metal (commodity) becoming an automobile (good). The exchange of goods enjoyed a lengthy market reign, but in turn, they were replaced as the dominant economic driver by the arrival of the service industry, which was essentially a product with value added. If we follow our example of metal being formed into an automobile, then an auto repair shop would represent the service level.

The service industry has enjoyed its own durable history as the defining market force, one that has continued into recent times. Modern economies, however, with their accelerated consumer demand and competitiveness, have evolved to want and need something more.

Service delivery is no longer enough; customers are now willing to pay – and pay well – for a new level of added value, one that includes an experience. In a competitive market, a car repair service that merely provides a mechanic and a service bay will struggle to survive without augmenting experiences such as a customer viewing platform, a manned snack bar, a waiting area with plasma TV, high-speed internet access with free Wi-Fi, a drive-thru option, at-home pickup or complimentary car rental. The Experience Economy, however, is not simply one of specialized or augmented services. To regard it as such would exclude the innovative and creative offerings that distinguish the Experience Economy from its predecessor. Certainly it is one thing to visit a wine store, purchase a few bottles, collect a few air miles while doing so and have the packages carried out to your car. It's something else altogether when the wine store features a top chef and his celebrity assistant to show you how to cook the food you can enjoy with that wine. Going back to Pine and Gilmore in *The Experience Economy:* "When a person buys a service, he purchases a set of intangible activities carried out on his behalf. But when he buys an experience, he pays to spend time enjoying a series of memorable events that a company stages – as in a theatrical play – to engage him in an inherently personal way."[8]

---

[8] B. Joseph Pine II and James H. Gilmore, *The Experience Economy*, (Boston: Harvard Business Review Press, 2011), 3.

I buy my suits from a local tailor, one of the last independently owned men's stores in my city of Ottawa. On a recent visit there, my consultant George pulled me into a private room to show me the results of recent renovations. The room was fabulously furnished and featured a wet bar among other things. George let me know that when I next return, this is where we will do my fittings – no longer in the main part of the store. It's a better experience, he tells me, and he's right. It's more in line with the attitudes and preferences of the store's clientele, he tells me, and he's right again.

THE IMPERATIVE FOR DELIVERING EXPERIENCES

It is a given in today's marketplace that the Experience Economy has arrived and is thriving. One need look no further than Walt Disney World Resort, Starbucks or the Genius Bar inside every Apple retail store to discover businesses that have ensured their economic strength and customer loyalty by providing exceptional connections and experiences.

Companies that are in the business of delivering experiences can point to clients who are advocates, economic growth through word-of-mouth, employees who are inspired, and durability during difficult economic times.

The Experience Economy is now the prevailing differentiator between those businesses which merely provide customers with what they've come to expect and those which engage customers in highly personal, memorable and engaging ways. The difference or gap between those two deliverables – what's known in the experience industry as "customer sacrifice" – is the one thing that business owners need to close if they plan on having any kind of longevity and growth. It would be a mistake – and a critical opportunity lost – to dismiss the relevance and applicability of the Experience Economy to one's business, regardless of the goods or services it happens to provide.

It would be a mistake, too, to assume that providing those you serve with an experience they will remember would require execution on the scale of Disney World or demand a significant budget. Nothing could be further from the truth. Just as some of our favorite personal memories involve kind words said or the smell of a pine tree, experiences are memorable not because of what they cost but because they engage us and we perceive them to be real.

Given this challenge to change, then, how does a business make the transition from being a provider of products or services to being the engineer of experiences that deliver to customers and clients those products and services in ways they really want?

MEETING EXPECTATIONS VS. EXCEEDING EXPECTATIONS

It's important to first know what customers truly are looking for. By understanding these expectations, business owners can then create experiences that can be transformative, both for their clients and for their own professional and corporate growth.

Value

In an environment where dollars change hands, it goes without saying that one of the first criteria that customers and clients look for is value. Unless your business is Walmart, however, value doesn't necessarily mean cheap. (Nor is that last statement meant to deride Walmart, which is memorable precisely because it delivers on low cost.) What is memorable to customers is something that is personally valuable. Whatever it is they are looking to buy – a product, service or experience – it has to connect with them as something that improves their own sense of worth.

Understanding

Customers want to be understood. They need to know that what they want is being met in ways that are important to them. A product must look, feel, taste, smell or sound a certain way. A service must be delivered personally, understandably, comprehensively and specifically to need.

Predictability

Customers need to know that what they will receive, either as a product, service or experience, will be consistently provided *every time*. There is only one Big Mac and one way of lining up for it, and customers know that they can get it anywhere in the world every time they step into or drive up to a McDonald's restaurant.

Involvement

Customers desire a heightened level of involvement in their business interactions. Being involved builds upon the sense of personal value (since no two people react to an experience the same way), turning a commercial transaction into an expected pleasure. Consider the following example: singer Katy Perry released her studio album *Teenage Dream* in the summer of 2010. When buyers opened the CD, they were met with the aroma of sweet cotton candy from an additive applied to the veneer of paper artwork housed within the jewel case. For consumers, their product purchase went from being an anticipated musical experience to one invoking adolescent memories of county fairs and fun. They slipped in their ear buds and hit the Play button having been predisposed to what would follow. It's a strategy no different from baking bread or putting vanilla on warm light bulbs before showing a house.

These small, seemingly unimportant features do not add to the experience – they create it.

Belonging

Customers appreciate being recognized as members of a select community, and they are not reluctant to pay for it. Special membership bestows a sense of uniqueness to the purchaser, and strengthens their commitment and allegiance to the business with whom they are engaged. Sound improbable? Not to someone carrying a gold customer card from Starbucks with their name in it, or a U2 or Red Hot Chili Peppers fan willing to spend upwards of $50 for a concert t-shirt. Membership does indeed have its privileges.

I fly over one hundred times per year, and I am a recognized top client of Air Canada. Air Canada does a lot of wonderful things for me that they would not do for most flyers. For example, if I am going to be late for a flight, I can call the concierge, who will print my tickets, fill out my customs form and have everything waiting for me in their office, which is conveniently located right next to gate security. I can think of a few occasions where this feature of our relationship saved me from a business catastrophe.

Even though Air Canada costs me more, I don't begrudge what I pay them. When I travel on their jets, I am rewarded for my loyalty. I am often greeted in airports by the concierge, or I am met when connections are tight. You can laugh at me all you want, but at the end of a long business trip, checking in at the Air Canada desk for the starting leg of my return journey is often the first step in feeling at home. Air Canada is much more than just an airline to me. I feel I belong there.

When I disembark from these Air Canada flights, I stay in Starwood Hotels whenever I can; their chain includes, among others, Westin, Sheraton and W Hotels. True, collecting points is a nice benefit, but it's the expedited check-in and flexible check-out that matter most to me. Whenever I stay with them, I am able to keep my bags in my room so that after a day of work, I can return to my hotel, slip off my suit and catch a later flight in comfortable clothes. To the non-business or non-frequent flyer, these perks may seem trivial. But to a person who travels throughout the year, these benefits are difference makers.

EXPERIENCE ENGINEERING 101: IMAGINE, INSPIRE, INNOVATE, ACCELERATE

Knowing what customers want, how then do business owners transform their companies and build experience delivery into the framework of their customer transactions?

It starts with accepting the inevitability of the Experience Economy, of being – to paraphrase the words of Tom Wolfe – either on the bus or not. Embracing its potential, as a first step, shows that you are at least willing to imagine how the transfusion of experiences into customer interactions can raise your corporate game.

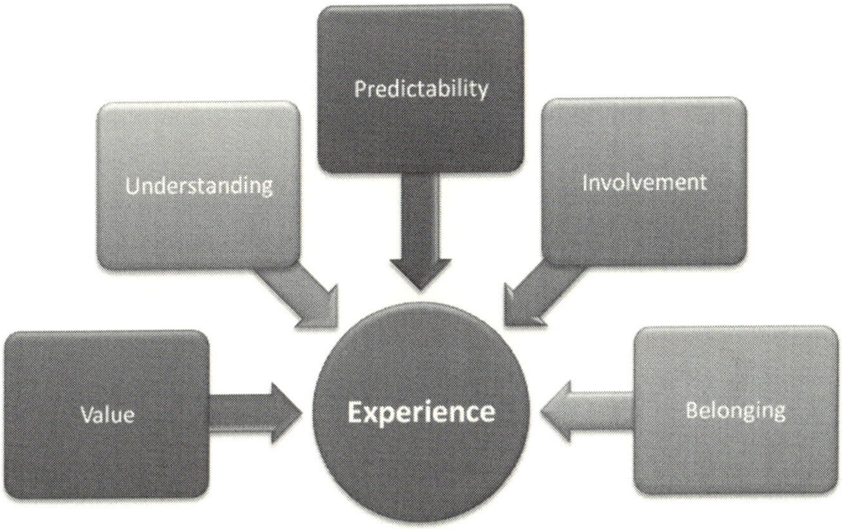

From imagination comes inspiration, fundamentally important because inspiration fuels everything that follows. A business owner who is inspired to change is a business owner open to possibilities, to finding the energy, creativity and entrepreneurial enthusiasm to move forward.

Part of that forward motion is examining and revamping, if necessary, corporate intent. This means that business owners don't merely wish to surpass their customers' expectations, but they feel they are obliged to. They regard every interaction with a customer as one that must reflect and communicate the customer's importance in order for the obligation to become fulfilled. The result is that customer interactions become proactive and controllable rather than reactive and beyond control. Employees brought into this process likewise feel empowered and enthused rather than insignificant and uninvolved. Delivering experience, as we can see, is a two-way door, infusing vitality to both sides of the customer relationship.

Think of the support staff who are part of the client onboarding experience we examined earlier. They are as involved in shaping the relationship, in looking for opportunities and in being empowered to make a difference, as every other member of the team. Think of restaurants where you are cared for by a floor service team rather than a single server. The tips are pooled and split, but each server in the group is responsible for you. You are never left waiting; whoever recognizes your need solves your problem.

Inspiration, in turn, leads to innovation. One need only look to the home entertainment industry to see how innovation has changed the viewing experience in the past twenty years and inspired still more innovation and greater customer experience. Opportunities for innovation on smaller scales are no less available. Whether one sells cookies or insurance, experience can be built into a company's offerings by examining each step of the delivery processes that already exist and weighing it against what customers want. Determining how each existing step might be improved upon from an experience-generating perspective leads to exploring new and additional experiences.

When I was about thirteen years of age, my cousin bought a yet-to-be-built home in Toronto that was scheduled for construction later that year. Still, he wanted us to see what he had purchased. He took my mom and me to a warehouse near the housing development. We all went inside where we were ushered into a movie theatre to watch a short film on the history of the builder, the company's attention to fine details, its craftsmanship, and so on.

When the film ended, the screen raised and the wall behind the screen slid open to reveal a neighborhood of model homes, completely furnished with cars in the driveway. Watch the film, walk into Stepford. We were able to see the home my cousin bought and tour it. Because I was still a kid, I remember being completely amazed that there were dishes on the shelves and clothes in the cupboard, like a giant dollhouse. This was at least thirty years ago, but my memory still holds the delight I felt by the surprise inside the seemingly ordinary warehouse.

Paramount to implementing any experience, however, is the need to keep it real. If not delivered authentically, experiences, by virtue of being constructed or staged, can be subject to consumer suspicion that the experiences are contrived or lacking in sincerity. Look back, however, on each example presented so far. Are there any in which the intention of the experience was not wholly transparent in how it engaged the customer personally and memorably? The experience of being immersed in a Disney theme park is highly staged, yet one would be hard pressed to suspect the corporate intent of being anything other than a sincere desire to deliver to their guests (never "customers") an authentic and well-intentioned experience. Again, sincerity of intent needs to be kept foremost in planning.

THE USUAL EXCUSES

Even with the Experience Economy percolating all around us, many business owners choose to ignore incorporating some aspect of it into their delivery. Four major reservations are expressed time and again.

What's it going to cost me?

We can tackle this a few ways. First, consider what it is going to cost you *not* to do it: customer disloyalty, uninspired employees, stagnant personal growth. Let's not forget the figure from the previous chapter about 77% of high net worth individuals indicating that the only way they will choose an advisor is via referral. The financial services industry does not operate in a bubble. It is not the only industry that is working in the experience economy. Thinking critically about the need to enhance the client experience isn't just a cute or convenient topic; it is essential to your very survival. A recommendation is the most cost effective avenue for growing an enterprise.

Each of these results has its own attendant costs. When clients aren't aligned with your offerings, the likely outcomes are a lack of referrals and poor word-of-mouth. Employees who are not inspired to engage customers in creative ways can tire of their routines, leading to diminished productivity, abuse of sick days and staff turnover. The same can hold true for the owner. Ask yourself this: is what one gets from the day truly more important than how one gets through it?

How much does it cost to dazzle? Surprisingly little, with a little imagination.

An advisor who once heard me speak told me that he wished he could innovate but felt he didn't have the money. One day, while grocery shopping (inspiration can strike anywhere – clean up in aisle 3!), an idea came to him. He had just picked up a case of bottled water for the office. After leaving the grocery store, he went across the mall to one of those dollar stores (the kind that used to be called a five and dime) where everything costs about a buck. He bought a few fancy glass bottles that had snazzy caps on them, the porcelain kind on a hinge. They looked very Old World and were pretty. When clients now come in for meetings, his assistant brings in these nice bottles of chilled water. "Everyone comments on them," he tells me.

Secondly, delivering experience IS marketing. What would be paid out in advertising, promotions and marketing otherwise? And to what effect? How compelling is broadcast advertising to customers who haven't already been predisposed through experience?

When you need to find a professional or a service or a great restaurant, where do you go? You go to people you know. And after that, where next? You go to the Internet.

A good friend of mine owns a gorgeous hotel. He asked me recently if I read my community newspaper. The reason for his question was because he was thinking of buying an ad. Personally, I couldn't imagine buying an ad in a community newspaper unless I were buying it to reassure my existing patrons that I was 1) still in business, and 2) doing well to be buying ads in community newspapers.

My advice would be, don't spend money trying to convince people who are not convinced.

What if he were to take the $3,000 he was willing to pay a community newspaper and instead pay a person to call all his known and existing clients just to say hello and to thank them for their continued support? What if he timed those calls in advance of a special season (Christmas, weddings, the Autumn colors)? Invest in the experience for your clients. Strive to make every moment, every step along the way inspirational and enjoyable.

Finally, customers are willing to pay for experience encounters. Whether the costs are embedded in product or service offerings (for example, a Starbucks coffee or an Apple iAnything) or whether a visible fee is charged (a rock band fan club membership), the Experience Economy is not a giveaway.

I choose to fly Air Canada even though Air Canada is more expensive. The better experience is worth it to me. Let me be clear: the ability to get on the airplane first so that I can stow my bag and become comfortable is worth thousands of extra dollars a year.

Status quo: I'm doing fine as is.

And maybe you are. Entrepreneurial risk doesn't appeal to everyone. Sometimes the timing is wrong for a business owner. Perhaps retirement is only a year away, or perhaps other events in the owner's personal life are placing demands on time and attention.

Or maybe you are just uninspired. I have met a lot of guys making $250,000 a year who are going through the motions. They are choosing not to innovate because they don't have to, not because they believe they shouldn't.

Avoidance of risk for the sake of avoidance, however, only leads to stagnation. Nothing is static, whether the company is Ford, Walmart or the shoe repair on the corner. The history of commerce abounds with examples showing that every sector of the economy is subject to a lack of innovation that can spell its demise, whether it sells commodities, goods, services or experience. Therefore, business owners would be well-advised in being proactive about creative innovation rather than reactive to market conditions.

Be brave! Think like an artist – you are creating something truly wonderful, and the little things can make the most difference. I once checked into a Four Seasons hotel in Washington, D.C. The Four Seasons believes in having an army of doormen handy, and they take a team approach to welcoming you. What I appreciated the most was the doorman who grabbed my bag and escorted me to the front desk. He asked me for my name and then announced to the front desk agent: "Mr. Moseley-Williams to check in." It's not that big a deal, is it? It helps set the tone for the entire experience of the hotel. I expect more and they charge more.

How authentic and sincere can anything be that is staged?

To quote Barry Tatelman, furniture salesman and Experience Economy entrepreneur, "There's no business that's not show business."[9] Customers are accustomed to staged experiences; in fact, they anticipate them strictly for the enjoyment they provide. Staged experiences succeed precisely because of the transparency of their intent.

Restaurateurs have long known that staged dining experiences are hugely successful despite their cost. In fact, the staging is often associated with the brand. It seems that people will gladly pay for the privilege of putting food in their mouths in unusual ways. Many consider it a rare treat to eat a meal prepared from 18th century recipes while dining in Salzburg's oldest restaurant as period-costumed singers and musicians perform Mozart by candlelight. Extend the specialty even further, and diners will gladly pay high sums months in advance for non-refundable *tickets* just so they may dine in Chicago's Alinea or Next restaurants where a sampling experience will easily set a person back $300 before the sommelier even waves a cork in one's vicinity. Green taffy balloons or pine needles in a phyllo pillow don't come cheap.

I don't have the staff.

Actually, you do. Up until now, however, you've probably been focusing on *what* they do – the activities they carry out and tasks they need to complete.

While these tasks are important, it is just as important, when delivering experiences, for your staff to focus on *how* they do the job. You may have a receptionist in your office, but what would be the impact upon clients arriving for a business meeting if your receptionist were to meet them in the lobby of your building, recognize them on sight with a warm handshake, and personally escort them to meet with you? Would your clients perhaps find that experience more personal, more engaging, more memorable?

---

9 Pine & Gilmore, *Experience*, 97.

WHERE DOES IT ALL LEAD?

In a word, it leads to acceleration. A business whose point of difference is to attract customers in predictable, engaging, novel, unexpected yet anticipated ways is one whose momentum sets it apart from those not yet on board with the Experience Economy. These energetic and creative enterprises ride the crest of the economy, enjoying the view from this new vantage, content to foster a sense of community in the economic niches they've carved out for their clients and themselves. Their goal is vibrancy – for themselves and for those whose business they've earned. Trust, transparency, engagement – these are not mere buzzwords of a new order. They represent the *raison d'être* of being in business, of forging strong relationships while reaping the results of one's labors.

In 1953, Walt Disney drafted a proposal to secure funding for the new theme park he envisioned. In it, he wrote: "I want to have a place [where] all the people in it are first-class citizens and treated like guests."[10]

As a business owner and employer, can your own purpose be very far removed from this same goal?

All you have to remember is to start.

---

[10] *Disneyland's History*, http://www.justdisney.com/disneyland/history.html, accessed April 2, 2013.

Recommended Reading, Surfing and Listening

Linchpin: Are You Indispensable? by Seth Godin.

A remarkable description of the role of those within organizations who are the glue, the catalysts, the hub. They create order out of chaos, excitement out of drudgery and art from the commonplace.

Do The Work by Steven Pressfield.

My introduction to the Lizard, that part of our brain that cooks up excuses, alibis, rationalizations, justifications, and every other reason to avoid what we know we really should be doing.

Outliers: The Story of Success by Malcolm Gladwell.

An examination, in ways we haven't considered, of what sets high achievers apart from the rest of us.

Blink: The Power of Thinking Without Thinking by Malcolm Gladwell.

Once again, Malcolm Gladwell proves that the mind is a wonderful thing. In this book, he examines how the 'adaptive process' – those rapid and unconscious mental processes that we call instinct and intuition – can serve or fail us.

The E-Myth Revisited: Why Most Small Businesses Don't Work and What to Do About It by Michael Gerber.

The classic treatise of step-by-step processes in building a successful business. Explores the notion that being an entrepreneur and being a manager don't necessarily equate.

The Starbucks Experience: Five Principles for Turning Ordinary into Extraordinary by Joseph Michelli.

People-driven philosophies and practices are at the heart of the Starbuck's success story. This book shows how adopting methods of these approaches can benefit every business.

The Experience Economy by B. Joseph Pine II and James H. Gilmore.

The seminal book on how the staging of client and customer experiences can transform a company into one that is unique and advocated. It's all here, folks.

One-Minute Manager by Kenneth H. Blanchard and Spencer Johnson.

A quick read about three important business basics: praise, correction and goals. Too short and sweet not to be included in this list.

Trust-Based Selling by Charles H. Green (audio).

Tips on building trust-based relationships with clients and closing sales.

The War Against the Chtorr by David Gerrold.

Does this series of four books (*A Matter for Men, A Day for Damnation, A Rage for Revenge, A Season for Slaughter*) have anything to do with business? Not really. But it's an excellent series and one I have to recommend. Go wiki it.

www.sethgodin.com

Seth provides more evidence that experience and permission marketing of remarkable offerings are the only ways to truly distinguish one's business from the rest of the rabble.

www.thehip.com

"I want a book that will make me drunk/Full of freaks and disenfranchised punks." – Gord Downey. The Tragically Hip have been the soundtrack of my life since I was about 15 years old. My life without them – and you – would be so much less. I hope you find some joy in there.

About the Author

DENNIS MOSELEY-WILLIAMS is an internationally known speaker and consultant to the financial services industry, specializing in the areas of practice management, business development and experience delivery. Since 1997, his primary business goal and passion has been to help advisors create sustainable, predictable, and process-driven practices through the integrated application of effective communications strategies and best business principles.

Dennis speaks to Fortune 500 companies at national conferences and works on retainer with individual clients and firms. His presentations teach the skills it takes to be successful in today's highly competitive world, and have established him as one of the industry's most popular speakers for keynote addresses and full-day workshops. He has a unique, passionate, and humorous style influenced by the lessons he learned working with top-flight advisors and entrepreneurs.

He is founder of Dennis Moseley-Williams Strategic Consulting, an innovative practice management company that helps organizations reach, connect with, and build sustainable positive relationships with their desired communities.

Dennis, his wife Sherri, their two daughters and their yellow lab, Smooch, live in Ottawa, Canada except during the summer months, when they are found in the western foothills of the Quebec's Laurentian Mountains, enjoying the pristine beauty of their cottage, Pine Lodge.

25667284R00113

Made in the USA
Charleston, SC
11 January 2014